The Saints' Guide to

MAKING PEACE WITH GOD,
YOURSELF AND OTHERS

The Saints' Guide to

MAKING PEACE WITH GOD,
YOURSELF AND OTHERS

Paul Thigpen

For Michael

God bless you, brother!

Paul Thigpen

Nov. 17, 2005

CHARIS

SERVANT PUBLICATIONS
ANN ARBOR, MICHIGAN

Charis Books is an imprint of Servant Publications especially designed to serve
Roman Catholics.

All Scripture quotations, unless indicated, are taken from the Revised Standard
Version of the Bible, copyright 1946, 1952, 1957. Catholic edition of the New
Testament © 1965. Catholic Edition of the Old Testament, incorporating the
Apocrypha, © 1966 by the Division of Christian Education of the National
Council of Churches of Christ in the USA. Used by permission.

Published by Servant Publications
P.O. Box 8617
Ann Arbor, Michigan 48107

Cover design by Paul Higdon - Minneapolis, MN

01 02 03 10 9 8 7 6 5 4 3 2 1

Printed in the United States of America
ISBN 0-56955-224-X

Library of Congress Cataloging-in-Publication Data

The saints' guide to making peace with God, yourself, and others /
[compiled by] Paul Thigpen.
    p. cm.
  Includes bibliographical references.
  ISBN 1-56955-224-X (alk. paper)
   1. Peace—Religious aspects—Catholic Church. 2. Christian saints.
3. Peace—Religious aspects—Catholic Church—Quotations, maxims, etc.
4. Christian saints—Quotations. I. Thigpen, Thomas Paul, 1954–

  BX1795.P43 S25 2001
  242—dc21

                            2001028658

*As St. Augustine asked his readers
to pray for his mother,
St. Monica,
I ask you to say a little prayer now
for my mother,
Margaret Thigpen,
to whom this book is dedicated
with all my heart.*

I neither see nor hear anything but the peace of God and all that pertains to it.... For peace's sake there is no trouble that I will not undertake, no act, no word of humility, that I will shrink from; no journey will be too long, no inconvenience too great, if only I may be rewarded by being able to make peace.

St. Basil
Epistles

CONTENTS

"BLESSED ARE THE PEACEMAKERS"
An Introduction

Now may the Lord of peace himself give you peace at all
times in all ways.

> St. Paul
> 2 THESSALONIANS 3:16

For peace is so great a good, that even in this earthly and
mortal life there is no word we hear with such pleasure,
nothing we desire with such zest, or find to be more thoroughly gratifying.

> St. Augustine of Hippo
> *City of God*

Not long ago I stumbled across the texts of the angry corre-
spondence that once flew furiously across the miles between
St. Jerome and St. Augustine. After fifteen centuries, the pages
still feel hot to the mind's touch: St. Jerome was known inter-
nationally for his prickly disposition; St. Augustine, for his
stormy passions. Their dispute was largely scholarly, but the two
men took it all quite personally—as scholars often do—so that
intellectual criticism might as well have been physical assault.

To make matters worse, rumors sailed faster than couriers between St. Jerome's hermitage in Palestine and St. Augustine's episcopal residence in North Africa. To each man came an earful of infuriating gossip about the other's alleged schemes and obstinacy. When the ancient equivalent of mail-service snarls caused long delays in the delivery of their letters (is anything new under the sun?), mutual suspicion and resentment sometimes boiled over into bitter accusations.

I found the scenario startling. Saints facing off with their fists up? Men with halos fuming and pouting and hurling not-so-subtle barbs at each other? We probably won't find *this* scene commemorated in stained glass! And yet we must remember that if the halos seem to be missing here, it's only because the halos were still in the making. In fact, it was precisely through such incidents that the saints learned just how valuable was the grace of peace—peace with God, with themselves, and with one another.

St. Augustine and St. Jerome, after all, eventually worked through their differences—the personal ones, if not the scholarly ones—and their friendship was salvaged. Out of the furnace of that fiery conflict they no doubt forged wisdom in how to deal righteously with adversaries. As with all the saints, God used such episodes to craft and polish their halos. He can do the same for us.

If such quarreling quills seem to us quite tame compared to the more serious conflicts we often face in life, we can be sure that in the stories of other saints we find models for dealing with much more grievous injuries. Read thoughtfully, for example, the humble, gracious prayer of St. Thomas More for his enemies and executioners, written in the shadow of the gallows as he awaited his martyrdom. Ponder the anguish of eleven-year-old St. Maria Goretti, lamenting the fate of her murderer and forgiving him even as she lay dying from his assault. In these remarkable scenes, so tragic and yet so full of faith, hope, and love, we're challenged to explore the profound depths of mercy that only the grace of God in Jesus Christ can make possible.

Here, then, is a modest collection of quotes and stories to help us forgive and be forgiven, each one reflecting some telling thought or experience of a saint who sought to make peace. The arrangement of topics follows a natural order flowing from common spiritual experience: first, peace with God, then, peace with ourselves, and finally, peace with others, each kind of peace being built on the one before it. The disorder within and around us that comes from sin, the saints have insisted, shatters our peace in all these relations, so we must repent and be reordered for tranquility to be restored.

With uncharacteristic verbal restraint, I've tried to keep my commentary in this volume to a minimum, allowing the saints to speak for themselves. I originally had gathered nearly three times as much excerpted material as you'll find in the finished book; after so much painful condensation, I couldn't bear to leave out any more of the saints' thoughts for the sake of presenting my own.

The majority of the excerpts reflect either my original translations or my modernizations of older texts in the public domain. In some cases I've taken considerable liberties in order to render the sense of the text. The textual sources are acknowledged in a list at the end of the volume. Occasionally an anecdote reported here is a composite drawing from multiple biographical accounts of a saint.

Many thanks to all the "usual suspects" for their support and assistance in compiling this work: in particular, Bert Ghezzi, Mary Graulich, Heidi Saxton, and all the fine folks at Servant whose labors and expertise have been indispensable; my wife, Leisa, and my children, Lydia and Elijah, for their patience and long-suffering; and all the friends who held me up in prayer during some rather trying family crises that occurred just as the work was being completed.

Pope John Paul II declared that the Jubilee Year just now ending would be a season of extraordinary grace, and so it was. With special indulgences the Church welcomed millions whose acts of penance demonstrated their sincerity in seeking divine forgiveness and making peace with heaven. Meanwhile, by publicly asking forgiveness for a multitude of injuries committed by Christians throughout history, the Holy Father brought us a step closer to finding that peace on earth among people of goodwill promised by the angels so long ago.

In the same spirit, I offer this compilation of saintly wisdom and example, with a prayer that readers will find here inspiration to seek and maintain peace with God, with themselves, and with others. The saints invite us all to learn firsthand the meaning of our Lord's glorious promise: "Blessed are the peacemakers, for they will be called children of God" (Mt 5:9, NAB).

Paul Thigpen

I.
PEACE WITH GOD

For even to be at peace with all men profits us nothing if we are at war with God. And in the same way, even if all men count us as enemies, it is of no harm to us if with God we are at peace.

St. John Chrysostom (c. 347-407)
Homilies on First Corinthians

ONE

"SEETHING LIKE THE SEA"
Our Need for Peace With God

For in [Christ] all the fulness of God was pleased to dwell, and through him to reconcile to himself all things, whether on earth or in heaven, making peace by the blood of his cross.

And you, who once were estranged and hostile in mind, doing evil deeds, he has now reconciled in his body of flesh by his death, in order to present you holy and blameless and irreproachable before him, provided that you continue in the faith.

St. Paul the Apostle
COLOSSIANS 1:19-23

How many are your mercies, O God—mercies yesterday and today, and at every moment of my life, from before my birth, from before time itself began! I am plunged deep in mercies—I drown in them: they cover me, wrapping me around on every side.

Venerable Charles de Foucauld (1858-1916)

"Peace," observes St. John Chrysostom, "is the mother of all good things." Is it any wonder, then, that a prayer for peace whispers—at times even shouts—throughout sacred history? *Shalom*, the ancient Hebrew greeting of peace, echoes throughout the Old Testament, in the mouths of priests and prophets, kings and warriors, herdsmen and farmers. The psalmists especially cry out for peace, and urge us all to pray for its reign.

In the New Testament, the theme of peace continues: St. Zechariah prophesies that the Dawn from heaven will come to "guide our feet into the way of peace" (Lk 1:79); when that Dawn arrives, angels announce his birth with a promise of peace on earth (see Lk 2:14). Later, as the Savior makes his way through a needy world, he repeatedly speaks peace to those who will listen and promises peace as his lasting gift (see Jn 14:27). Then, after his death, resurrection, and ascension, his apostles repeat the blessing as they scatter across the face of the earth, bringing hope that peace can be found in him.

Yet, to find peace, we have to know exactly what it is that we're seeking. Is peace simply the absence of conflict? Or is it something much more rich, full, and alive?

What Is Peace?

St. Augustine of Hippo (354-430), a brilliant bishop and Doctor of the Church, spent most of his early years as a spiritual wanderer, tossed by incessant interior storms, longing desperately for peace. After he found his rest at last in God, he gave considerable thought in his later years to the nature of peace. As St. Augustine saw it, true peace is a kind of harmony, much like a sweet, vibrant musical chord composed of varying yet complementary tones. When differing elements—body and soul, parent and child, neighbor and neighbor, God and humanity—come together in concord, each in its appropriate role and place, the result is peace.

The peace of the human body consists in the function of its parts according to their proper arrangement. The peace of the lower part of the soul—our appetites—is found when these appetites rest in harmony. The peace of the higher part of the soul—our reason—depends upon the harmony of our actions with what we know to be true. The peace of body and soul with each other is the well-ordered and harmonious life and health of the living creature.

Peace between man and God is found in the well-ordered obedience of faith to eternal law. Peace between man and man is well-ordered concord. Domestic peace is the well-ordered harmony between those of the family who rule and those who obey. Civil peace is a similar harmony among the citizens. The peace of the heavenly city—the city of God—is the perfectly ordered and harmonious enjoyment of God, and of one another in God.

Order is the arrangement that sets things equal and unequal in their rightful places. The peace of all things, then, is the tranquility resulting from such order.

The City of God

Sin Shatters Peace

If peace with God comes from living in harmony with his will, then sin can only shatter our peace. For sin is a deliberate turning away from God, a rebellion against his authority, a disordering of our relationship with him. Those who resist God thus make themselves the enemies of God. "'There is no peace,' says the Lord, 'for the wicked'" (Is 48:22).

In his celebrated spiritual autobiography, The Confessions, *St. Augustine tells of his youth in rebellion against God. He observes how the torment of sin can force us to recognize that we are broken and disordered, pressing us to seek a restoration of the peace we so profoundly desire.*

I was a poor fool, seething like the sea. Forsaking you, Lord, I followed the violent course of my own torrents. I rushed past all your lawful bounds, and I did not escape your scourges. For what mortal can escape them? But you were always beside me, mercifully angry, ruining all my illicit pleasures with bitter discontent—all to draw me on so that I might instead seek pleasures that were free from discontent. But where could I find such pleasures except in you, Lord? I could find them only in you, who teaches us by sorrow, and wounds us in order to heal us, and kills us so that we may not die apart from you....

You humble the proud, who are like those wounded. Through my own bloated pride I was separated from you; yes, my face was so swollen that my eyes were shut and blinded. Yet even though you, Lord, are the same forever and ever, you do not remain angry with us forever. For you take pity on us, who are only dust and ashes. It was pleasing in your sight to transform what was deformed in me; and by inward stings you disturbed me, so that I would be dissatisfied until I could see you clearly with the eye of my soul. By the secret hand of your healing my swelling was relieved; and the disordered and darkened eye of my mind was day by day made whole by the stinging salve of a healthy sorrow.

The Confessions

God by His Nature Is Merciful

If our sins have wrecked our peace with God, how is that peace to be restored? How can the enemies of God become his friends? We're morally and spiritually bankrupt, in debt to him, and we're too weakened by our disordered state to right the wrong. Only God himself, then, can forgive us the debt, heal the wounds of our relationship with him, and reconcile us to himself. Yet is he willing to do so?

The saints have answered that question with a thunderous "Yes!" God is "rich in mercy" (Eph 2:4), insisted St. Paul (d. c. 67). His desire is reconciliation.

St. Faustina Kowalska (1905-38) has come to be known as "the Apostle of Divine Mercy." A member of the Congregation of Sisters of Our Lady of Mercy in Poland, her life was consumed by a desire to convince the entire human race that God is eager to forgive us and bring us back into communion with himself. Her diary records what the Lord said to her.

Tell the whole world of my great mercy.... Mankind will not have peace until it turns with trust to my mercy.... Proclaim that mercy is the greatest attribute of God. All the works of my hands are crowned with mercy....

Let no soul fear to draw near to me, even though its sins be as scarlet. My mercy is so great that no mind, be it of man or of angel, will be able to fathom it throughout all eternity. Everything that exists has come forth from the very depths of my most tender mercy. Every soul in its relation to me will contemplate my love and mercy throughout eternity.

You see what you are of yourself, but do not be frightened at this. If I were to reveal to you the whole misery that you are, you would die of terror. However, be aware of what you are. Because you are such great misery, I have revealed to you the whole ocean of my mercy....

Speak to the world about my mercy; let all mankind recognize my unfathomable mercy. It is a sign for the end times; after it will come the day of justice. While there is still time, let them have recourse to the fount of my mercy; ... I am giving mankind the last hope of salvation; that is, recourse to my mercy.

Divine Mercy in My Soul

God's Offer of Peace: Jesus Christ

How does God extend his mercy to us? St. Paul proclaimed that "we have peace with God through our Lord Jesus Christ," his divine Son, having been "reconciled to God by [his] death" (Rom 5:1, 10). Yet how could this death and resurrection accomplish our "atonement"—which means literally our "being made one"—with the God against whom we have rebelled? St. Alphonsus Liguori (1696-1787), bishop, missionary, and Doctor of the Church, tells us how Christ can be our mediator with God.

We must remember that for this very end our Redeemer came upon earth, that he might pardon sinners: "The Son of Man came to save that which was lost" (see Mt 18:11).... By dying, Jesus desired to regain for God all mankind who were lost. Oh, how great is the debt we owe to Jesus Christ!

If a criminal condemned to death were already standing at the gibbet with the rope around his neck, and a friend were to come and take the rope, and bind it round himself, and die in place of the guilty man, how great would be his obligation to love him! This is what Jesus Christ has done; he has been willing to die on the cross to deliver us from eternal death....

Man, by reason of his sin, was a debtor to the divine justice, and an enemy of God; the Son of God came on earth and took man's flesh; and thus, being God and man, he became a mediator between God and man, acting on behalf of both; and in order that he might bring about peace between them, and obtain for man the divine grace, he offered himself to pay with his blood and his death the debt due by man.

The Passion and Death of Jesus Christ

St. Cyril of Jerusalem (c. 315-86) was an outstanding catechist who became bishop of the ancient city where Jesus died and was resurrected. In his series of lectures to those who sought entrance into the Church, he explored the theme of Christ's sacrifice by explaining that our Lord had solved what had constituted a divine dilemma: How could God accomplish both justice and mercy on behalf of the sinful human race?

These things the Savior endured, and made peace through the blood of his cross, reconciling to himself all things, whether in heaven or on earth [see Col 1:20]. For we were enemies of God through sin, and God had justly ordained that the sinner must die. So one of two things had to happen: Either God, being true to his word, had to destroy all men, or else in his mercy he had to cancel the sentence of death.

But behold the wisdom of God: He preserved both the justice of his sentence and the exercise of his mercy. Christ "bore our sins in his body on the tree, that we might die to sin and live to righteousness" [1 Pt 2:24].

Of no small account was the One who died for us. He was not a literal sheep; he was not a mere man; he was more than an angel; he was God made Man. The great transgression of sinners could not match the even greater righteousness of the One who died for them. The great sin we committed could not match the even greater righteousness that was worked by the One who laid down his life for us—who laid it down when he pleased, and took it up again when he pleased.

Catechetical Lectures

St. John Chrysostom, a reforming patriarch of the great city of Constantinople, marvels at the great grace of peace with God that comes through Jesus Christ—a gift far beyond anything we could deserve or even understand.

"And the peace of God, which passes all understanding, will keep your hearts and your minds in Christ Jesus" [Phil 4:7]. What does this mean? "The peace of God" that Christ has made possible toward men surpasses all our understanding.

For who could have expected, who could have hoped, that such good things would have come to us? What God has done exceeds, not just anything we could say, but even anything we could understand. For God's enemies, for those who hated him, for those who determined to turn themselves away from him— for these, he refused nothing, not even to give up his only-begotten Son, so that he might make peace with us.

This is the peace, then, this is the reconciliation, this is the love of God, that will guard your hearts and your thoughts.

Homilies on Philippians

No Sin Is Too Great

So God the Father offers us peace through forgiveness in his Son. Yet what if we have serious sins in our past? Will God still forgive us and welcome us? Is his mercy great enough to pardon even the worst of crimes?

St. Augustine answers these questions pointedly: If God could pardon even the murderers of his own beloved Son, is there any sin he can't forgive?

The Apostle's Creed says, "I believe in the forgiveness of sins." ... Let no one say, "I've committed this or that sin: maybe it won't be forgiven me." Just what sin have you committed? Just how great a sin was it? Name any heinous crime you've committed—heavy, horrible, which you shudder just to think about—whatever sin you choose. But tell me: Have you killed Christ?

No deed could be any worse, because no one could be better than Christ. What a dreadful thing it would be to kill him! Yet afterward many who had killed him believed on him and drank his blood in the Eucharist. So even they were forgiven the sin they had committed.

On the Creed: A Homily to the Catechumens

Recognizing Our Need for Forgiveness

While some of us hesitate to seek God's forgiveness because we think our transgressions are too great, others of us have the opposite problem: We fail to recognize the sins we have, thinking we have no need to seek peace with God. St. Bridget of Sweden (1303-73) was a fearless mystic and visionary whom God often used to rebuke sinners in high places who failed to recognize their sinfulness. When she visited the royal court in Naples in 1372, she daringly spoke Christ's words in the first person—a sharp prophetic warning that severely rebuked the sins of those at court, yet offered them forgiveness.

O my enemies, why do you so boldly commit sins and do other things contrary to my will? Why have you neglected my passion? Why don't you pay attention in your hearts to how I was stretched out naked on the cross and cried out, full of wounds and clothed in blood?

But your eyes and hearts forget and neglect all these things. And so you behave like prostitutes, who love the pleasures of the flesh, but not its offspring. For when they feel a living infant in their womb, at once they procure an abortion so that without losing their fleshly pleasure, they may always engage in their foul intercourse.

You behave in just the same way! For I, God, your Creator and Redeemer, visit everyone with my grace, knocking at your hearts, because I love all of you. But when you feel at the door of your hearts any knocking of my Spirit, or any compunction, or when through hearing my words you conceive any good intention, at once you procure a spiritual abortion. You excuse your sins and delight in them; you're even willing to persevere in them until you're damned! For that reason, you do the devil's will, contemptibly taking him into your hearts while throwing me out.

But this is the greatness of my mercy: None of my enemies is so complete or so great a sinner that I would deny him my forgiveness if he were to ask for it humbly and wholeheartedly.

The Revelations

If we doubt our need for deliverance from sin, and our desire for the peace that such deliverance gives, we need only look into our hearts, says St. Augustine, and witness the disorder of our passions fighting against our conscience. What we find will press us to seek God's forgiveness.

Everyone who feels within himself his fleshly desires rebelling against the right inclinations of conscience—who feels the habit of sin, with unrestrained violence, dragging him into captivity—should recall to mind as much as he can what kind of peace he has lost by sinning. Then he will cry out like the apostle Paul, "O wretched man that I am! Who will deliver me from the body of this death? I thank God through Jesus Christ" [see Rom 7:24-25].

In this way, when he cries out that he is wretched, in the very act of lamenting his sins, he begs the help of a Comforter. And he has made no small progress toward blessedness when he has come to know his own wretchedness; that is why Jesus said, "Blessed are those who mourn, for they shall be comforted" [Mt 5:4].

On the Sermon on the Mount

If we need a further incentive to seek God's forgiveness, St. Augustine suggests we should consider the alternative: Hell, after all, is the final, logical outcome of sin, the horrifying state achieved by souls when grace no longer sets any limits to their disorder.

If war is the opposite of peace, as misery is the opposite of happiness, and life is the opposite of death, it's reasonable to ask what kind of unending war will be the fate of the wicked corresponding to the everlasting peace that, as we have noted, is the destiny of the righteous. The person who raises this question has only to observe what it is in war that is hurtful and destructive—I mean, of course, nothing else than the conflict of things mutually opposed.

Can we conceive a more grievous and bitter war than one in which a person's will is so opposed to his passions, and his passions to his will, that their hostility can never be terminated by the victory of either? A war in which the violence of pain is in such conflict with bodily nature that neither one yields to the other? For in this life, when this conflict has arisen, either pain conquers and death brings the sensation of pain to an end, or else nature conquers, and health brings an end to the suffering. But in the world to come, the pain continues so that it torments, and the nature endures so that it feels the pain; and neither one ceases to exist—lest punishment should also cease.

The City of God

To spurn God's forgiveness, then, is to propel ourselves toward that nightmare of everlasting chaos awaiting the damned, a never-ending disintegration in which the human personality dissolves into countless warring lusts—the utter negation of peace.

TWO

"LOOK TOWARD THE THRONE OF INFINITE MERCY"
Our Response to God's Offer of Peace

If we confess our sins, he is faithful and just, and will forgive our sins and cleanse us from all unrighteousness.

St. John the Evangelist (c. 6-c. 104)
1 JOHN 1:9

When the apostle Paul says, "Let us have peace with God," he means, "Let us sin no more, nor go back to our former sinful condition." For that would be making war with God.

St. John Chrysostom
Homilies on Romans

God reaches out to us in Jesus Christ to restore us to his friendship. If we're honest with ourselves, our lack of peace convinces us of our need for forgiveness and reconciliation with our Creator. We then find ourselves asking the same question men and women have asked ever since the crowds in Jerusalem were convicted of their sin by the preaching of St. Peter: "What shall we do?" (Acts 2:37).

St. Peter's answer to the crowd rings down through the centuries: "Repent!" (v. 38). His apostolic comrade, St. Paul, repeated the admonition wherever he preached, telling all who would listen that they should "repent and turn to God and perform deeds worthy of their repentance" (Acts 26:20). Reconciliation is a two-way street: To be at peace with God, we must turn back to him, agree with him, and bring our lives into harmony with his will.

Confession and Penance

To "confess" means literally "to say the same thing." Confession is thus a matter of saying about ourselves the same thing God says about us: agreeing with him about the disorder of our sin, about the judgment we deserve from his justice, and about our need for his healing mercy. Penance means being sorry for our sin and wanting to change our ways—and it means taking concrete actions that will lead to the changes we desire.

If, then, we want to accept God's offer of forgiveness, acting with a faith that truly trusts in his mercy, we must confess and repent; we must admit our sin and turn away from it.

St. Fulgentius of Ruspe (468-533) was an African bishop and abbot who tirelessly wrote and preached the gospel of God's mercy, inviting his readers and listeners to confess and repent.

Thoughts about the wickedness of any particular sin shouldn't cause anyone to despair of the mercy of God. On the other hand, no one should keep on sinning on the pretext of hoping for the mercy of God when he dies. Instead, a hopeful person should confidently seek out the harbor of penance without faltering so that his humility may avoid the deadly shipwreck of despair.

He should love God's mercy in such a way that, although

fearful, he will take into consideration his justice as well. He should hope confidently that everything can be forgiven him when he turns from his sin. But let him keep in mind that nothing is forgiven a stubborn person who refuses to turn from his sin. So the wicked person ought to change his life now so that he won't suffer God's punishment.

Whoever doesn't wish to suffer endless misery must seek the mercy of the Lord. Whoever doesn't wish for eternal death must seek eternal life. Whoever doesn't wish to be damned with eternal punishment must hurry to confess before the face of God. For now is the time when penance bears fruit. Now is the forgiveness of sins granted to the person who does penance. Now is the time when those who turn to God are not denied a place in the kingdom of heaven, in which we will live and rejoice without end.

Works

Confession is necessary for peace with God, St. Augustine reminds us, because we can't live in harmony with him if we don't agree with him.

Do you want to see God? Then first you must confess, so that within yourself you make a place for God; because "his place is in peace" [see Ps 76:2 Douay-Rheims]. As long as you refuse to confess your sins, in a way you are still quarreling with God. Can't you see that you're arguing with him when you give your approval to what he disapproves of?... Since you are disputing with God, you haven't made for him a place in your heart, because his place is in peace.

So how do you begin to have peace with God? Begin with confession.... Begin by joining in agreement with the Lord. In what way?.... He detests your wicked life; if you love such a life, then you are separated from him. But if you detest it as well, then you are united to him through your confession.

Exposition on Psalm 76

St. Francis de Sales (1567-1622), a French missionary bishop and leader of the Catholic Reformation, was known for his practical wisdom as a confessor who stressed that holiness is possible in everyday life. He has offered a model prayer of confession and repentance.

Standing before the presence of the Eternal God and his heavenly host, I have reflected on the boundless mercy of his divine goodness toward me—his weak, unworthy creature, whom he has created out of nothing, preserved, sustained, delivered from so many dangers and loaded with so many gifts. Above all, I have considered the incomprehensible mercy and compassion with which this good God has endured my iniquities, inspiring me with good desires, winning me on to reform, and waiting so patiently until now for my repentance. He has done this all in spite of my ingratitude, disloyalty, and faithlessness, which have delayed my conversion and despised his grace, thus offending him....

Now at last coming to myself, prostrate in heart and soul before the throne of his justice, I own, acknowledge, and confess that I am thoroughly convicted of treason against God. I am guilty of the death and suffering of Jesus Christ, through the sins that I have committed and for which he died, enduring the cross. Therefore I consider myself worthy of death and damnation.

But I look toward the throne of infinite mercy of this same

Eternal God. Detesting the sins of my past life with all my heart and my strength, I humbly beg pardon and mercy and entire absolution of my sins, through the merits of the death and suffering of this same Lord and Redeemer of my soul. Resting on him as the sole foundation of all my hopes, I ... renounce the world, the flesh, and the devil, abhorring their hateful vanities, lusts, and passions, now and forever.

And turning to my compassionate and merciful God, I desire, intend, resolve, and earnestly dedicate myself to serve and love him now and for all eternity. I will seek his pleasure, devoting and consecrating my mind with all its faculties, my soul with all its powers, my heart with all its affections, and my body with all its senses, to his service. I resolve never again to pervert any part of my being to disobey his will and Sovereign Majesty, to which I spiritually immolate and sacrifice myself, intending to be always his faithful and obedient child, without hesitation or change.

If, however, through some human infirmity or the power of the enemy I should in any way compromise this, my steadfast resolution, I now declare that through the grace of the Holy Spirit I will return the moment I perceive my error, once more offering myself to the divine mercy without reservations or delay. This is my will, my intention, my inviolable and irrevocable resolution, which I profess and confirm without exception or reserve in the sacred presence of God, before the Church triumphant in heaven and the Church militant on earth....

Be pleased, O Eternal God, omnipotent and merciful Father, Son, and Holy Spirit, to confirm my resolutions and accept favorably this, my heart's offering. And as it has pleased you to give me the desire and will to serve you, give me also grace and strength to do so. O God, you are the God of my heart, my soul, and my spirit: I will acknowledge and adore you now and for all eternity. Amen.

Introduction to the Devout Life

Don't Delay

Are you convinced that you need to accept God's offer of peace? Then don't put it off until tomorrow, St. Augustine reminds us, because you don't know whether you'll even have a tomorrow.

Those who have any fear of God at all won't fail to reform themselves in obedience to his words—unless they're assuming that they still have a long time to live. But this very assumption causes so many to perish. For while they are saying, "Tomorrow, tomorrow," suddenly the door is shut....

Maybe you're saying to yourself, "God has promised me forgiveness; whenever I repent, I'll be secure; I've read it in the Bible: 'In the day that the wicked man turns away from his wickedness, and does what is lawful and right, I will forget all his iniquities' [see Ez 18:21-22]. I am secure, then; whenever I reform myself, God will give me pardon for my evil deeds...."

Well, what you say is true; God has indeed promised forgiveness when you repent; I can't deny it. But even if I grant that God has promised you pardon, who has promised you a tomorrow? If you find it in the Bible that you'll receive pardon when you repent, now read to me from the Bible how long it is that you have to live. Of course you must admit that you cannot read it there.

You don't know, then, how long you have to live. So reform

yourself; only then will you be always ready to die. Don't live in fear of judgment day, as if it were a burglar who will break into your house as you sleep [see Lk 12:39-40]. Instead, wake up and repent today. Why do you put it off till tomorrow?

Homilies on New Testament Lessons

Maintaining Peace With God

Once our friendship with God has been restored, if we want to remain at his side we must walk in step with his will. Continuing obedience, then, is the foundation for maintaining peace with God, because disobedience breeds disorder and, ultimately, separation.

Pope St. Leo I (d. 461) earned the title "the Great" for his highly successful, energetic administration of the Church in troubled political times, as well as his crucial role in clarifying authentic Christian teaching in times of doctrinal controversy. His homilies are models of clarity, laying out in simple terms the profound implications of theological truths.

Peace is what brings forth the sons of God; it's the nurse of love and the mother of unity; the rest of the blessed and our eternal home. The proper function and special mission of peace is to join to God those whom it removes from the disorder of the world. That's why the Apostle Paul encourages us toward this goal in saying, "Being justified therefore by faith, let us have peace with God" [see Rom 5:1]. In this brief sentence nearly all the commandments are summed up. For wherever true peace is, there can be no lack of virtue.

But what is it, dearly beloved, to have peace with God, except to desire what he bids us to do, and not to desire what he forbids us to do? In human friendships we seek those with souls like our own whose desires are similar to ours, and differences in habits keep people from ever attaining full harmony with each other. If that's the case, then, how can someone be a partaker of God's peace if he's pleased with what displeases God and delights in what he knows offends God?

That's not the spirit of the sons of God; such a way of thinking is unacceptable to the noble family of his adopted children. That chosen and royal race must live up to the dignity of its rebirth, must love what the Father loves, and in nothing disagree with its Maker. Otherwise, the Lord might have to say once more, as he did long ago, "Sons I have reared and brought up, but they have rebelled against me. The ox knows its owner, and the ass its master's crib; but Israel does not know me and my people have not acknowledged me" [see Is 1:2-3].

Those who have peace with God, who are always saying to the Father with their whole hearts, "Thy will be done," can never be overcome in battles with the devil, can never be hurt by his assaults. For in accusing ourselves in our confessions, and refusing to let our spirit consent to our fleshly desires, we stir up against us the enmity of him who is the author of sin, but secure a peace with God that nothing can destroy.

Sermons

In two homilies, St. Augustine reflects on the necessary relationship between peace and the righteousness that comes from obeying God. The two are inseparable, he insists—how, therefore, can we hope for peace if we don't love righteousness? On the other hand, if we seek to be righteous, we'll make the joyful discovery that the fruit of holiness is peace (see Heb 12:11).

"Mercy and truth have met each other: justice and peace have kissed" [Ps 85:10, Douay-Rheims]. Act righteously, and you will have peace, so that righteousness and peace may kiss each other. For if you don't love righteousness, you won't have peace, because those two, righteousness and peace, love one another, and kiss one another, so that whoever has acted righteously receives the kiss of peace.

Peace and righteousness are friends. Perhaps you desire the one but not the other: For there is no one who doesn't desire peace, but not everyone desires righteousness. Ask all people, "Do you wish for peace?" and with one mouth the whole race of man answers you: "I long for it, I desire it, I will to have it, I love it!" Well, then, they should love righteousness as well, for these two, righteousness and peace, are friends; they kiss one another. If you don't love the friend of peace, peace itself will not love you, nor even come near you.

Exposition on Psalm 85

Perhaps St. Columbanus (c. 540-615), the great Irish missionary monk, sums up these insights most succinctly: "Nothing," he concludes, "is sweeter than the peace of conscience."

THREE

"AT WAR WITH OUR VICES"
Recovering Peace When We Stumble

Create in me a clean heart, O God, and put a new and right spirit within me. Cast me not away from thy presence, and take not thy holy Spirit from me. Restore to me the joy of thy salvation, and uphold me with a willing spirit.

PSALM 51:10-12

We should seek God with determination and diligence and without sloth, as well as we can, through his grace, and we should do so gladly and merrily, without unreasonable depression and vain sorrow. It belongs to the proper goodness of our Lord God to excuse man courteously.

Blessed Julian of Norwich (c. 1342-1423)
Showings

The saints knew, perhaps better than most of us, how often we fall to temptation, how easily we let things come between God and ourselves. Life with the Lord is a daily struggle. Paradoxically, we must make constant war in order to obtain a lasting peace.

Yet we're not alone in the battle. "My grace is sufficient for you," God told St. Paul, "for my power is made perfect in weakness" (2 Cor 12:9). The saints have a great deal to say about how we can open ourselves to that divine grace and power.

Hope in the Struggle

A perpetual war against sin is better than a false peace resulting from compromise with sin, notes St. Augustine. Our struggle should give us hope—it's a sign, after all, that we're no longer content to be ruled by our passions.

For just as by the sin of one man, Adam, we have fallen into a misery so deplorable, so by the righteousness of one Man, who also is God, shall we come to a blessedness far beyond all we can conceive. Nor ought anyone to trust that he has passed from the one man to the other until he will have reached that place where there is no temptation, and have entered into the peace that he seeks in the many and various conflicts of this present war, in which "the flesh lusts against the spirit, and the spirit against the flesh" [see Gal 5:17].

Now, such a war as this wouldn't even exist if human nature had, in the exercise of free will, continued steadfast in the righteousness in which it was created. But now in its misery it makes war upon itself, because in its blessedness it would not continue at peace with God. Nevertheless, in this conflict, even though it's a miserable calamity, we're better off than we were before, when we failed even to recognize that a war was to be waged.

For it's better to struggle with our vices than it is to be at peace with them because they have conquered us. Better, I say, is war with the hope of everlasting peace, than captivity without any thought of deliverance. We long, indeed, for an end to this war and, kindled by the flame of divine love, our hearts burn to enter into that well-ordered peace in which whatever is inferior will forever be subordinated to what is superior. But even if (God forbid) there had been no hope of so blessed a fulfillment, we would still have preferred to endure the hardness of this conflict rather than, by our failure to resist, to yield ourselves to the dominion of vice.

The City of God

The effort to maintain peace with God thus demands a frequent reliance on repentance, a turning back to God again and again. Yet we must not lose hope, says St. Catherine of Genoa (1447-1510). This Italian mystic, whose early years were characterized by frequent calls for repentance, spent much of her later life listening to God's private revelations about the tenacity of his love for us.

When the soul is in sin, God does not cease to urge and inwardly call it. And if it responds to his gentle wooings, he receives it back into his gentle grace with the same pure love as before. He has no wish to remember that he has ever been offended, and he never ceases to show it all the benefits he can.

Purgation and Purgatory

Sacraments and Spiritual Disciplines

In practical terms, how do we respond to what St. Catherine called God's "gentle wooings"? When we recognize that we've turned away from God in some area of our lives, how do we go about turning back to him? The saints agree that grace to change can come to us through the sacraments and through traditional spiritual disciplines.

The Sacrament of Reconciliation

We can best begin our journey of repentance through the sacrament Christ has provided just for that purpose. As the *Catechism of the Catholic Church* observes, it goes by many names, each one emphasizing an aspect of what it helps to accomplish in our lives: the sacrament of *conversion,* the sacrament of *confession,* the sacrament of *forgiveness,* the sacrament of *reconciliation* (see par. 1423-24). In light of its role in restoring us to friendship with God, we should no doubt call it the sacrament of *peace.*

St. Thomas Aquinas (c. 1225-74) was a brilliant but humble Dominican friar whose theological and philosophical work has shaped the teaching of the Church for more than seven centuries. In his analysis of the Sacrament of Reconciliation, he compares confession to asking a doctor for help or coming into court for judgment.

If you want a physician to be of assistance to you, you must make your disease known to him. But it is necessary for salvation that man should take medicine for his sins. Therefore it is necessary for salvation that man should make his disease known by means of Confession.

Furthermore, in a civil court the judge and the one who stands accused are two different people. Therefore the sinner, who is the accused, ought not to be his own judge, but should be judged by another person—and consequently, should confess to another person.

Summa Theologica

That wisest of confessors, St. Francis de Sales, gives practical advice on how to keep our relationship with God healthy through the Sacrament of Reconciliation.

Our Savior has left in his Church the Sacrament of Penance and Confession, in order that as often as our souls are stained with sin we may cleanse and purify them. Since then you have so sure and simple a remedy at hand, never permit your heart to remain long stained by sin.... The soul that has consented to sin should abhor its condition, and hurry to be cleansed, remembering that the eternal eyes of God are watching. Why should we die a spiritual death when we have such a powerful remedy at hand?

You should make your confession humbly and devoutly once a week, always if possible before receiving Holy Communion, even if your conscience isn't burdened with any mortal sin. For by confession you receive not only absolution for the venial sins you confess, but also great assistance for avoiding them in the future, new light to discern them, and abundant grace to win back the ground you have lost because of them. Further, you practice the virtues of humility, obedience, simplicity, and love, so that by your act of confession you exercise more virtues than by any other means.

Always entertain a sincere hatred of the sins you confess, even if they are trifling, and a heartfelt resolution to change. Some confess their venial sins only mechanically and out of mere habit. Since they don't really think about correcting them, they continue in them, thus losing the opportunity for much spiritual good. If, therefore, you make an untruthful confession through lack of thoughtfulness, hurried words, or self-indulgence, repent earnestly and resolve firmly to change—for it is an abuse of the confessional to confess any sins, whether venial or mortal, without intending to get rid of them.

Don't be satisfied with general, vague confessions: "I haven't loved God as much as I should; I haven't prayed earnestly enough; I haven't shown my neighbors the charity I owe them," and so forth. For by such confessions you fail to enlighten your confessor about the true state of your conscience, since all the saints now in paradise—and in fact, every living person on earth—might confess the same.

Instead, examine what particular reason you have for accusing yourself of these faults, and having determined what it is, accuse yourself honestly and simply of that particular sin of commission or omission. For example, perhaps you say you haven't treated your neighbors with the charity you owe them because, having seen a poor man in great need whom you might easily have helped, you neglected to do so. Well, then, specify your neglect. Say, "I saw a needy brother and, either through indifference or hardness of heart" (as the case may be) "I refrained from assisting him...."

Again, don't content yourself with confessing the mere fact of venial sins, but mention as well the motive behind the sin. Thus, instead of simply confessing that you've told a lie that didn't hurt anyone, say whether you lied because of vanity—in order to protect yourself from blame or to win praise—or whether it was from thoughtlessness or perversity.... In addition, tell how long you persisted in your sin, for the longer you persist, the worse the sin is....

Be careful also to mention those details that explain the nature of your fault, such as the cause that excited your anger or led you to encourage someone in wrongdoing.... By thus honestly confessing everything, you not only disclose your actual faults, but also the bad inclinations, habits, and similar roots of sin that lurk within you. By this means your spiritual father obtains a more perfect knowledge of the heart he has to deal with and of the treatment to be prescribed.

Introduction to the Devout Life

The Eucharist

The saints have often expressed their gratitude for receiving Jesus' precious Body and Blood in terms of the peace it brings to the soul. It is "instant peace and balm to every wound," *says St. Elizabeth Ann Seton (1774-1821), an American convert who felt drawn to the reserved Host in the tabernacle long before she ever became Catholic. It is* "an island of peace in the ocean of the world," *observes St. Paul of the Cross (1694-1775), an Italian missionary brother who devoted his life to preaching about the passion of Christ, which reconciled us to God.*

We shouldn't be surprised that the Most Blessed Sacrament brings peace. After all, it was at the first Eucharist that Jesus promised to give us his peace (see Jn 14:27). The unspeakable gift of the divine sacrifice, bringing peace with God, was a restoration of our friendship with him—for "greater love has no man than this, that a man lay down his life for his friends" *(Jn 15:13).*

St. Peter Julian Eymard (1811-68), a French Marist provincial and preacher, established several religious congregations and other organizations dedicated to spreading devotion to the Blessed Sacrament. He saw in the Eucharist the culmination of God's long-suffering efforts to bring us back to himself.

God took four thousand years to prepare the reconciliation of man, which was to be perfected only in the Eucharist. The

Incarnation greatly advanced this work of regaining man's confidence, but it was not enough.... Could the Incarnation, work of salvation though it was and a sublime testimonial of the love and power of God, suffice to establish the confidence of friendship between the Creator and his creature? No, friendship demands constant personal intercourse. Therefore, our Lord instituted the Most Holy Eucharist....

Now, here is a sinner who has committed every kind of crime. He confesses; his wounds are bound up, and his convalescence begins. He feels a constant sadness; his conversion has made him more sensitive, and he bewails now what before he did not feel: the sorrow he has caused to God.... "I have sinned so greatly against God, who is so good!" he says to himself.

If he is left to himself, sorrow will overwhelm him, and the devil will drive him to despair. But have him go to Communion; let him but feel God's goodness within him, and joy and peace will spread through his soul.

"What!" he will say. "I have received the Bread of angels! Then am I not the friend of God?" His past sins trouble him no more in this moment. Has not our Lord himself told him that he is forgiven? And how can he doubt his word?

Holy Communion

Examination of Conscience

When the Anglican church leader Venerable John Henry Newman (1801-90) became England's most famous Catholic convert, he brought to his new faith the lively awareness of sin and its consequences so common in the evangelical Protestant tradition. Here he reminds us that we can't experience divine forgiveness if we don't have a clear sense of our personal need for it. Only a regular examination of conscience can keep us from a false sense of peace with God.

All those who neglect the duty of habitual self-examination are using words without meaning. The doctrines of the *forgiveness* of sins, and of a *new birth* from sin, cannot be understood without some right knowledge of the *nature* of sin, that is, of our own hearts.... Unless we have some just idea of our hearts and minds and of sin, we can have no right idea of a Moral Governor, a Savior, or a Sanctifier.... For it is in proportion as we search our hearts and understand our own nature, that we understand what is meant by an Infinite Governor and Judge; in proportion as we comprehend the nature of disobedience and our actual sinfulness, that we feel what is the blessing of the removal of sin, redemption, pardon, sanctification, which otherwise are mere words....

Men are satisfied to have numberless secret faults. They do not think about them, either as sins or as obstacles to strength of faith, and live on as if they had nothing to learn.... [But] if you have not even thought about your real state, nor even know how little you know of yourselves, how can you in good earnest be purifying yourselves for the next world, or be walking in the narrow way?

These remarks may serve to impress upon us the ... danger to which we are exposed, of speaking peace to our souls, when there is no peace.

Secret Faults

Daily Prayer

St. Cyprian of Carthage (c. 200-258) knew all too well that even the most sincere of believers could stumble; during the Roman imperial persecution of the Church under Decian, he witnessed the apostasy of many Christians who renounced their faith rather than face torture and death. In his commentary on the Our Father, St. Cyprian reflects on our need to pray daily, "Forgive us our debts." St. Augustine's thoughts on the same prayer expand those insights.

After this we also beg mercy for our sins, saying, "And forgive us our debts, as we also forgive our debtors." After asking for daily bread, we ask for pardon of sin, so that the one who is fed by God may live in God, and that not only the present, fleeting life may be provided for, but also the eternal life to which we may come if our sins are forgiven.

These sins the Lord calls debts, as he says in his Gospel, "I forgave you all that debt, because you asked me" [see Mt 18:32]. And how necessary, how provident, how beneficial it is to be reminded that we are sinners, since we are compelled to beg mercy for our sins. And while we ask pardon from God, the soul recalls its own consciousness of sin! So that no one might flatter himself that he is innocent, and by exalting himself be lost even more deeply, he is instructed and taught that he sins daily, in that he is commanded to ask mercy daily for his sins.

In addition, John, in his epistle, also warns us, saying, "If we say we have no sin, we deceive ourselves, and the truth is not in us. If we confess our sins, he is faithful and just, and will forgive our sins" [1 Jn 1:8-9]. In his epistle he has combined both truths: that we should ask mercy for our sins, and that we will obtain pardon when we ask for it. He said the Lord was faithful to forgive sins, meaning that he is faithful to his promise; because the One who taught us to pray for our debts and sins has promised that his fatherly mercy and pardon will follow.

St. Cyprian of Carthage
Treatise on the Lord's Prayer

Witness the prayer of the whole city of God in its pilgrim state, for it cries to God by the mouth of all its members: "Forgive us our debts as we forgive our debtors." And this prayer is effective not for those whose faith is "without works and dead" [see Jas 2:17] but for those whose faith "works by love" [see Gal 5:6].

Our reason, though subjected to God, is still "weighed down by the perishable body" [see Wis 9:15] as long as it is in this mortal condition. It lacks complete authority over vice; therefore this prayer is needed by the righteous. For even though our reason exercises authority, the vices don't submit without a struggle.

However well we maintain the conflict, and however thoroughly we have subdued these enemies, there steals in some evil thing that, even if it doesn't find ready expression in our actions, will slip out in our words, or insinuate itself into our thoughts. Consequently, our peace can't be full as long as we are at war with our vices. For the outcome of the conflict is uncertain; and even our victory over the vices we've defeated isn't secure, but full of anxiety and effort.

Amid these temptations, then ... who but a proud man can presume he is living in such a way that he has no need to say to God, "Forgive us our debts"?

St. Augustine of Hippo
The City of God

Having entered now into God's perfect peace in heaven, the saints themselves stand in the best possible place to help us maintain peace with God. As the friends closest to his heart, they desire, perhaps even more than we ourselves do, that we too might spend eternity as friends of God. St. Bridget of Sweden reminds us that the Mother of God especially, now our mother as well, is ready to intercede for us. "There is no sinner in the world," *she insists,* "however much he may be at enmity with God, who does not return to him and recover his grace, if he has recourse to Mary and asks her assistance."

St. Gregory Thaumaturgus (c. 213-68), the missionary bishop of Pontus whose second name means "wonder worker," experienced a vision of the Blessed Mother—the earliest such apparition for which any record survives. His prayer to Our Lady emphasizes her role in helping us find God's peace.

You have been made the mother of him who is at once Judge and Redeemer. Hail, you stainless mother of the Bridegroom of a world bereaved!... Hail, you living temple of God! Hail, you who gave a home to heaven and earth alike!...

Through her has come the Physician to heal the sick; for those who sit in darkness, the Sun of righteousness; for all who are tossed and beaten by storms, the Anchor and the Port undisturbed by any tempest.

For the servants who had become irreconcilable enemies of God, the Lord has been born—the One who sojourned with us to become the bond of peace and the Redeemer of those led captive, the peace of those who had been hostile to God.

For he is our peace; and may it be granted to us all that we may enjoy that peace, by the grace and kindness of our Lord Jesus Christ; to whom be the glory, honor, and power, now and forever, and unto all the ages of the ages. Amen.

Homilies on the Annunciation to the Holy Virgin Mary

FOUR

"A PRESS OF TROUBLE"
When Adversity Endangers Our Peace With God

*When my soul was embittered, when I was pricked in heart,
I was stupid and ignorant, I was like a beast toward thee.
Nevertheless I am continually with thee; thou dost hold my
right hand.*

PSALM 73:21-23

*Without the burden of afflictions it is impossible to reach the
heights of grace. The gifts of grace increase as the struggles
increase.*

St. Rose of Lima (d. 1586)

Whatever else we may say about the Psalms, we must admit that
they're honest—sometimes painfully, embarrassingly so.
Screams of anguish, whispers of doubt, shouts of triumph, even
cries for revenge all find their place in these telling "mirrors" of
the soul, as St. Athanasius (c. 297-373) called them.

At times the psalmists make the startling admission that
they're angry with God. They even have the audacity to scold
him: "Lord, don't hide your face when I'm in trouble!... Hurry
up and answer me when I'm talking to you!" (see Ps 102:2).
They question sarcastically his wisdom and concern: "Just how
long, Lord, will you let my enemies scoff at me? Do you plan to

let those people despise you forever? Why are you sitting on your hands?" (see Ps 74:10-11). They accuse him of neglect: "My God, my God, why have you abandoned me?" (see Ps 22:1).

In these lively complaints, no doubt the psalmist-saints are often only speaking out boldly for the rest of us. In times of adversity, we, too, may be angered by what God has done or failed to do. We may feel hurt, confused, and afraid. If God is truly all-powerful and all-loving, we may think, then why am I in such a mess? He can do whatever he wants to do. Why doesn't he help me? In fact, why did he let this happen in the first place?

If we hold on to such anger, we come to bear a grudge against God. Our friendship with the Lord is thus fractured—not so much because we've offended *him*, but because he's offended *us*.

The saints had more than their share of adversity, and an ample share of annoyance at heaven as well. Yet they came to recognize that being *offended* by God wasn't the same as being *wronged* by God. God never wrongs us. Yet, it's possible to take offense at what he does or fails to do, because we don't always understand his purposes.

Tough times, then, become a sterling opportunity to grow in faith. We can choose to trust God's wisdom and care as the most faithful of friends, though he may seem to be absent or even hostile. Or we can choose to bear resentment against God—and shatter our peace with him.

Adversities Versus Offenses

Adversity becomes an offense—a stumbling block—in our relationship with God only when we allow ourselves to be scandalized by it. If we trust that our Lord knows what's best for us, says St. Augustine, troubles may press us, but they won't oppress us.

Take careful note of what "offenses" are: It's not the adverse circumstances of this life that are called offenses—that is, things that cause us scandal. Consider, for instance, the man who under some hard necessity is weighed down by a press of trouble. The simple fact that he is weighed down with a press of trouble is no offense to him. After all, by such pressures the martyrs were pressed—but they weren't *oppressed*.

Beware of an offense, but don't fret yourself over the press of troubles. Troubles only press you, while an offense oppresses you. What then is the difference between the two? In the press of trouble you prepare yourself to maintain patience, to hold firm, refusing to abandon faith or consent to sin.

If you're able to do this, the trouble that presses you won't cause you to fall. Instead, that press of trouble will have the same result as an oil press, whose purpose isn't to destroy the olive, but to extract the oil. In a word, if in this trouble that presses you, you give praise to God, how useful will the press be to you—the means by which such oil is pressed out! Under such a press the apostles sat in chains, and in that press they sang a hymn to God [see Acts 16:23-25]. What precious oil was this that trouble pressed and forced out!

Beneath a heavy press Job sat on the dunghill, without recourse, without help, without substance, without children; full, but of worms only—that is, as far as the outward man was concerned. But because he too was full of God within, he praised God, and that press was no offense to him.

Where then was the offense, the stumbling block? When his wife came to him and said, "Curse God, and die" [Job 2:9]. When everything else had been taken from him by the devil, and Eve was left behind for the sufferer, not to console but to tempt her husband.

See then where the offense was. She exaggerated his miseries, and her miseries along with his, and tried to persuade him to blaspheme. But he ... had "great peace" in his heart, as the psalmist says, because he loved the law of God, and nothing could make him stumble, nothing could be an offense to him [see Ps 119:65]. She was an offense, but not to him. "You speak," he said, "as one of the foolish women would speak. If we have received good from the hand of the Lord, shall we not bear the evil?" [see Job 2:10].

Homilies on New Testament Lessons

Lack of Earthly Goods

The psalmist confesses: "My feet had almost stumbled, my steps had well nigh slipped. For I was envious of the arrogant, when I saw the prosperity of the wicked.... All in vain have I kept my heart clean" (Ps 73:2-3, 13). Here he identifies a common source of resentment toward God: our perception that we aren't being sufficiently rewarded for obeying him. We compare ourselves to those whose material possessions are greater than ours, and if their way of life is questionable, we wonder why God seems to favor them over his own.

In ancient Constantinople, St. John Chrysostom served a vast and mixed congregation of the rich and poor, the powerful and powerless. In this homily he reproves his flock for questioning God's distribution of earthly goods. As we read his rebuke, we should keep in mind that this wise teacher is speaking out of the strong conviction, shared by all the ancient Church fathers, that wealth is morally and spiritually dangerous—that, as Jesus taught, it's easier for a camel to squeeze through the eye of a needle than for a rich man to enter the kingdom of heaven (see Lk 18:24-25).

On the other hand, he also insists that poverty is nothing to be ashamed of, and that the lack of material goods need never harm our souls in any lasting way. In fact, we can turn such lack to spiritual advantage by trusting God to provide for us.

"All these are given by one and the same Spirit, apportioning to each one individually as he wills" [see 1 Cor 12:11]. "Let's not, I beg you, feel cheated," says St. Paul; "nor should we complain, saying, 'Why have I received this and not that instead?'" Nor should we call the Holy Spirit to account for his choice of gifts.

For if you know that whatever God has chosen for you was given according to his providential care, then consider that the same care has determined how much you've received. So be content and take pleasure in what you've received—don't complain about what you haven't received. Instead, admit that God has favored you by not giving you things you couldn't handle.

And if in spiritual gifts we ought not to be questioning God's judgment, much more is that the case in material goods. We should be quiet and refrain from coyly inquiring why one person is rich and another poor.... Why was Abraham rich while Jacob lacked even bread? Weren't both of them righteous?

Didn't God say concerning both of them, "I am the God of Abraham ... and of Jacob"? [see Ex 3:6] Why then was the one a rich man, and the other a hired servant?...

Why? Because it was expedient for each one to be in their particular circumstances. That's why with regard to each one, our conclusion must be, "Thy judgments are like the great deep" [Ps 36:6]. For if those great and wonderful men weren't treated the same way by God—but one was given poverty, and another riches; one was given ease, and another trouble—then how much more ought we now to bear these things in mind....

Of course, we could account for these things by saying that poverty has no power to hurt a righteous man—in fact, to be righteous despite poverty is a high honor. Meanwhile, the bad man in his riches possesses only a hoard of punishment stored up for the future, unless he repents. In fact, even before judgment day, often his riches will become to him the cause of many evils, and lead him into ten thousand pitfalls. Nevertheless, God permits it, both to demonstrate that the man is freely exercising his will, and to teach others not to be crazy in chasing after money.

"Why is it then," you may ask, "that a wicked man may be rich and suffer nothing dreadful?... Well, even in this situation he is to be pitied. For wealth added to wickedness only aggravates the mischief.

Is he a good man, but poor? Well, nothing has injured him. Is he a bad man, but poor? Then he deserves to be poor; in fact, his poverty can be to his advantage.

"But what if he received his riches from his ancestors," you may say, "and now lavishes it on prostitutes and parasites—yet he doesn't suffer any evils?" Just listen to what you're saying! He fornicates with prostitutes, and yet you say, "He doesn't suffer any evils"? He's a drunkard, and you think he's at ease? He spends his money to get into trouble, and you consider him someone to be envied?

No! For what can be worse than a wealth that destroys the very soul? If his body were twisted and maimed, you would weep bitterly for him. Yet you see his whole soul mutilated— and you still count him happy!...

Isn't it ridiculous that Christians who expect to live forever and to inherit the good things that "no eye has seen, nor ear heard, nor the heart of man conceived" [1 Cor 2:9] should strive after and envy things that will be left behind on earth when we die?... If, on the other hand, you say you know these things, then stop busying yourself with questions about the reasons why one person is rich and another one poor. You might as well ask why one person is light-skinned and another dark, or one person hook-nosed and another flat-nosed. For just as these other things should make no difference to us, neither poverty nor riches should matter.

In the end, everything depends on how we use our possessions. If you're poor, you can still live cheerfully through self-denial. If you're rich, you're the most miserable of all men if you flee from virtue. For this is what really concerns us: matters of virtue. If we aren't virtuous, everything else is useless.

Homilies on First Corinthians

On the same theme, St. Augustine adds the reminder that as faithful Christians we need not envy the prosperity of the wicked if we learn to value rightly the spiritual riches we have.

One man is prosperous, another man toils; the one lives wickedly and yet is prosperous, the other lives rightly and is distressed. The one who lives rightly and is in distress must not be angry; he has within himself the virtue that the prosperous man lacks. So he shouldn't be sad or trouble himself or give up. That prosperous man may have gold in his treasure chest, but the righteous man has God in his conscience.

Compare the two: gold and God, treasure chest and conscience. The one man has what perishes, and has it stored up where it will perish; the other man has God, who cannot perish, and has him where he can never be taken away—if only he is upright in heart.

Homilies on the Gospel of St. John

Physical Infirmity

A second significant cause of resentment against God is ill health or disability. St. Syncletice (fourth century), abbess of a monastic community in the deserts of ancient Egypt, was revered both for her wise counsel and for her holy austerity. We need not resent God when we suffer physical illness, she teaches; it can actually be a spiritual medicine.

If you're troubled by sickness, don't be sad.... We need these adversities to put to death the desires of the flesh. In fact, they serve the same purpose as fasting and other forms of physical austerity. If your senses are dulled by sickness, for example, you need not fast.

Just as a powerful medicine cures a sickness, so sickness itself is a medicine to cure the passions. And the soul profits a great deal by bearing sickness quietly and giving thanks to God. If we go blind, we must not be disturbed. Though we have lost one means of achieving spiritual excellence, yet we can contemplate God's glory with the interior eyes of the soul. If we go deaf, we must remember that we will no longer hear a lot of frivolous talk. If suffering has weakened our hands, we still have an inner strength against the devil's assaults. Even if the entire body should be afflicted with disease, the health of the inner man is still improving.

Sayings of the Fathers

Taking Offense at God's Law

A third cause of resentment against God is our failure to understand and appreciate the laws by which he expects us to live. Why, we may ask, does God have so many rules? When those rules keep us from doing what we want to do, we may take offense. St. Augustine warns that if we take offense at God's law, then we haven't yet learned to love his will or trust his wisdom.

"Great peace," the psalmist says, "have those who love thy law; nothing can make them stumble" [Ps 119:165]. Does this mean that the law itself is not an offense—a stumbling block—to those who love it, or that there is no offense from any source for those who love God's law?

Actually, both senses are rightly understood. For the one who loves the law of God honors in it even those parts he doesn't understand; and when something in it seems to him to sound absurd, he concludes instead that he must not understand it, and that there must be some great meaning hidden in it. Thus the law of God is not an offense to him.

Exposition on Psalm 119

Adversity Is God's Surgery

Do we hold a grudge against our doctor for causing us pain when it's necessary for our cure? Of course not! Nor should we resent the Great Physician, says St. John Chrysostom, for subjecting us to treatment that brings discomfort in this life in order that we can be whole in the next.

The physician is not to be commended only when he leads the patient into gardens and meadows, or refreshes him in baths and pools of water, or sets before him a well-furnished table. No, he's also to be commended when he orders the patient to refrain from food and drink; when he oppresses him with hunger and lays him low with thirst; when he confines him to his bed, making his house a prison and depriving him of the sunlight by shadowing his room on all sides with curtains. Even when he cuts, and when he cauterizes, and when he administers his bitter medicines, he is still a physician.

Isn't it then preposterous to call the one who does so many evil things a healer, and yet blaspheme God, and deny his providence, if he ever does one of these things to us? And yet he is the only true physician both of souls and bodies. On this account he often seizes this nature of ours as it suffers fits of prosperity, travailing with a fever of sins. Then, by deprivation, and hunger, and death, and other calamities—all the medicines he knows how to use—he frees us from our diseases.... For he is full of resources, and the medicines he prescribes for our salvation are manifold.

Homilies on the Power of Demons

A Sense of Humor

A final practical tip from the saints will help us to avoid getting angry at God: When trouble comes our way, it helps to have a sense of humor.

St. Teresa of Avila (1515-82), the great Spanish mystic, Carmelite reformer, and Doctor of the Church, was known for her quick tongue and biting wit. One day she was making a rather difficult journey, traveling in a cart, to found a new convent. While fording a river, the cart overturned, and St. Teresa tumbled into the cold water. After she got up with what little dignity she could muster, her companions heard her pray: "Lord, if this is how you treat your friends, no wonder your friends are so few!"

II.
PEACE WITH OURSELVES

Wherever you are, remember me, and pray for me that no cause of disturbance may dwell in my heart, and that I may be at peace with myself and with God.

St. Basil
Epistles

FIVE

"LET THIS WAR BE ENDED"
Healing the Soul in Conflict With Itself

For I delight in the law of God, in my inmost self, but I see in my members another law at war with the law of my mind and making me captive to the law of sin which dwells in my members. Wretched man that I am! Who will deliver me from this body of death? Thanks be to God through Jesus Christ our Lord!

St. Paul
ROMANS 7:22-25

Peace, peace, the Lord said, my sisters.... Well, believe me, if we don't find peace in our own house, we'll not find it outside. Let this war be ended.

St. Teresa of Avila
The Interior Castle

St. Teresa of Avila, the first woman to receive the revered title of Doctor of the Church, merited that honor in part because of her profound teaching on the inner workings of the soul. Her insights stemmed from her conviction—shared with saints through the ages—that theology was inseparably entwined with psychology. "We'll never completely know ourselves," she wrote to one acquaintance, "if we don't strive to know God." Her observation is complemented by the assertion, also common among the saints, made by St. Cyprian: "If you want to know God, you first have to know yourself."

In her great mystical work *The Interior Castle*, St. Teresa likens the soul to an inner fortress with many rooms. The castle is our home, and the goal is to make God at home there as well, in every nook and cranny. Yet that process is a complicated one, and too often what should feel like a welcoming celebration begins to feel more like armed resistance to a siege.

The search for peace, St. Teresa insists, begins at home, in that interior castle of the soul. "What hope can we have of ever finding rest outside of ourselves," she asks, "if we can't find rest within?"

Sin Disorders the Soul's Inner Workings

Just as sin makes us enemies of God, it makes us our own worst enemies. The saints have long pointed out that there's a rightful and necessary chain of command in creation, with God as Creator and Designer at the top, our human reason and will under him, and our animal nature under that. When we submit our higher, rational nature to God, our lower, irrational nature submits to us. When we rebel against God, however, rebellion spreads through the ranks, and we find ourselves facing resistance from the powerful interior forces we were meant to govern.

St. Dionysius of Alexandria (d. 265) was an Egyptian bishop, theologian, and biblical scholar. His fifteen years as head of Alexandria's world-famous catechetical school before his consecration as bishop gave him ample opportunity to elaborate an understanding of sin's effects on the soul.

For when people set themselves either to do evil or to do good to others, what they do is certainly not confined to the carrying out of their will on those others. For to the degree that they attach themselves to iniquity or to goodness, they will themselves become possessed either by divine virtues or by unbridled passions.

Those possessed by virtue will become the followers and comrades of the good angels. Both in this world and in the other, with the enjoyment of perfect peace and immunity from all ills, they will fulfill the most blessed destinies for all eternity, and in God's fellowship they will possess forever the supreme Good—God himself. But those possessed by their passions will fall away at once from the peace of God and from peace with themselves. Both in this world and after death they will abide with the spirits of vengeance.

On the Reception of the Lapsed to Penance

This inner war, notes St. John Chrysostom, is in some ways worse than the conflicts pitting individuals or even nations against each other. For those who fight in the latter kind of battle may flee the battlefield; but how is it possible to escape from ourselves?

There are three very serious kinds of war. The first is public, when our soldiers are attacked by foreign armies. The second comes when even in time of peace we are at war with one another. The third occurs when the individual is at war with himself, which is the worst of all.

For war with a foreign power has no power to inflict the worst kind of injury. So what, I ask you, if we should even be killed? That doesn't injure the soul.

Neither does the second kind of war have power to harm us

against our will. For even if others are at war with us, we our-
selves can be at peace with them. That's what the prophet says:
... "With them that hated peace I was peaceable" [Ps 120:7,
Douay-Rheims]....

But from the third kind of war we find only a risky escape.
For if the body contends with the soul, and raises an army of evil
desires, and arms against it with sensual pleasures or the evil passions of anger and envy, we can't attain the promised blessings
until this war is brought to an end. Whoever fails to calm this
tumult will fall, pierced by wounds that will bring the death that
awaits in hell.

For that reason, we must take great care every day that this
war may not be stirred up within us; or short of that, if it's
stirred up, that it may not last, but be quelled and put to sleep.
For what advantage is it to us, if the whole world enjoys profound peace, but we are at war with ourselves?

This, then, is the peace we should strive to keep. If we have
it, nothing from outside of us will be able to harm us.... But if
we're disturbed inside even when everything around us is at
rest, we are miserable creatures indeed.

Homilies on First St. Timothy

*The same repentance from sin that brings peace with God will
lead to peace with ourselves. We must recognize our need for grace
to quell the inner war, St. Augustine says, and cry out to Jesus
Christ.*

If you have begun to follow God, you'll find strife inside you.
What strife, you ask, will you find? "The desires of the flesh are
against the Spirit, and the desires of the Spirit are against the
flesh" [Gal 5:17].

Look: You may be alone, but you are still with yourself. You may not be fighting with anyone else, but you see within yourself another law warring against the law of your mind, and taking you captive to the law of sin that's in you.

Cry out, then, and cry to God, so that he may give you peace from the inner strife: "Wretched man that I am! Who will deliver me from this body of death?" Only the grace of God through our Lord Jesus Christ.

Homilies on the Gospel of St. John

Forgiving Ourselves

Having been our own worst enemy, we've injured ourselves many times. Sometimes we fail to find interior peace because we've failed to forgive ourselves for those self-inflicted wounds of the past. Yet if God has forgiven us, who are we to refuse forgiveness to ourselves?

The saints of the ancient desert monastic communities had plenty of time to think about the past, and sometimes such thoughts could disturb their peace. In his youth, St. Pambo (d. c. 390) was a disciple of St. Anthony of the Desert (251-356), the austere, holy Egyptian hermit celebrated as the father of Christian monasticism. Seeking peace, young Pambo once asked the old man, "What should I do?" St. Anthony replied with laconic wisdom: "Don't trust in your own righteousness. And don't keep doing penance for a deed that is past and gone."

St. Clement of Alexandria (c. 150-c. 215), like St. Dionysius a director of the famous catechetical school of ancient Alexandria, emphasized God's mercy to his catechists. Because nothing we have ever done is beyond God's forgiveness, he insists, repentance has two aspects: turning away from sin, and turning away from preoccupation with the past.

For the Scripture says there is great, abundant joy and festivity in heaven among the Father and his angels when one sinner turns and repents [see Lk 15:7]. For that reason God cries out ... "I desire not the death, but the repentance of the sinner" [see Ez 33:11]. "Though your sins are like scarlet, I will make them white as snow; though they are blacker than darkness, I will wash and make them like white wool" [see Is 1:18]....

The Lord commands us each day to forgive our repenting brothers. And if we, "being evil, know how to give good gifts" [see Mt 7:11], how much more is it the nature of the Father of mercies, the good Father of all consolation, full of pity and pardon, to be long-suffering and to wait for those who have turned! For to repent is actually not just to cease from our sins, but to stop looking behind us.

Who Is the Rich Man That Shall Be Saved?

To keep us humble, God may allow us to recall the failures of the past. Yet because of his grace, St. Augustine shouts in this joyful prayer, that past now has no power over us. Our sins have melted away.

"What shall I render to the Lord?" [Ps 116:12]—for even though he recalls to my memory the sins of my past, my soul isn't made fearful by them! Lord, I will love you, and thank you, and confess to your name, because you have put away from me so many evils and so many wicked deeds. To your grace I attribute it, and to your mercy, because you have melted my sins as if they were ice.

Confessions

Faith in God's mercy, then, allows us to let go of the past, to forgive ourselves and to make peace with ourselves. St. Gemma Galgani (1878-1903) was a young Italian mystic who endured considerable adversity in her brief life: consumption by spinal tuberculosis, demonic assaults, and the scorn of family and neighbors who jeered at her visions of Christ. Her heroic life of faith modeled this prayer of confidence in God's grace: "If I saw the gates of hell open and I stood on the brink of the abyss, I would not despair, I would not lose my hope of mercy, because I would trust in you, my God."

SIX

"THOSE POISONOUS LITTLE REPTILES"
Threats to Peace With Ourselves

*Why are you cast down, O my soul, and why are you disqui-
eted within me? Hope in God; for I shall again praise him,
my help and my God.*

PSALM 42:5-6

*A man must be lenient with his own soul in his weaknesses
and imperfections, and put up with his own failings in the
same way he puts up with those of others. But he must not
become idle and must encourage himself to better things.*

St. Seraphim of Sarov (1759-1833)

"Those poisonous little reptiles," St. Teresa of Avila called them—
tiny, creeping spiritual pests in the "interior castle" that feed on our
unwillingness to appreciate forgiveness in all its fullness. We act impa-
tiently with ourselves, failing to realize that we must forgive ourselves
just as we must forgive others. We scrupulously fret over our own
failings, trying to take God's place as the judge of our souls. If such
merciless habits push us too far into self-condemnation, we lose
confidence even in God's mercy, and we sink into despair.

If we want to preserve interior peace, we have to send these
pesky critters running. The remedy? In one form or another, the
saints agree on two spiritual pesticides—humility and faith.

Impatience With Ourselves

Surely one of the greatest threats to interior peace is our impatience with ourselves. When unchecked, this tendency can degenerate into a bitterness characterized by self-contempt—an ironic form of pride. What we need, then, is humility—that is, the maintenance of an accurate self-estimate. We must recognize our own limits. "It's unfair," *observed St. Frances de Sales,* "to require from ourselves what is not in ourselves to give."

Be gentle with yourself, this wise confessor urged those under his spiritual direction. You must be as patient and long-suffering with yourself as you would be with anyone else.

One of the forms in which we should practice gentleness regards ourselves, in never growing irritable with ourselves over our imperfections. For although it's reasonable for us to be vexed and angry with ourselves when we commit faults, yet we ought to guard against a bitter, fretful displeasure or spiteful anger with ourselves. Some make a great mistake in being angry with themselves over the fact that they have been angry, hurt over the fact that they have been hurt, and vexed over the fact that they have been vexed.

In this way they imagine that they are ridding their hearts of anger, and that their second passion remedies the first. But they are actually preparing the way for a fresh anger at the first opportunity that presents itself. Besides this, all this indignation and vexation and irritation with ourselves tends to foster pride and springs entirely from self-love, which is displeased at finding that we are not perfect.

We should endeavor, then, to look upon our faults with a calm, collected, firm displeasure. A judge who passes sentence thoughtfully and calmly punishes vice more effectively than if he is impetuous and hasty, for if the latter is true, his punishment is determined more by his own feelings than by the nature of the crime committed. In the same way, we correct ourselves more effectively by a quiet, persevering repentance than by an irritated, hasty, passionate repentance. For the latter is carried out more according to our impulse than according to the seriousness of our faults....

Believe me: The corrections of a father will have much greater effect upon his child if they are offered kindly and gently than if they are hot and angry. In the same way, when we have erred, if we reprove our heart gently and calmly, pitying it rather than reproaching it, and encouraging it to reform, its repentance will be much deeper and firmer than if we are angry, stormy, and irritable.

For instance, if I particularly desired not to yield to the sin of vanity, yet nevertheless I fell seriously into it, I would not begin to say to my heart, "Aren't you wretched and abominable to be carried away by vanity after so many good resolutions! You ought to die of shame, and not even presume to lift up your eyes to your God, you blind, insolent, faithless traitor!"

Instead, I would seek to correct it by reasoning and compassion in this way: "My poor heart, here we are fallen into the very trap we have so often resolved to escape! Come on—let's get up again and never fall in it again. Let's call for God's mercy and put our trust in it, because it will help us to stand firmer in the future so we can return to the path of humility. Let's not be discouraged, but instead be on our guard from this time on. God will help us and guide us."

By such reproof I would establish a firmly rooted resolve not to fall again into the same fault. And I would then take such steps as seem advisable, and as my spiritual director would suggest, in order to keep from falling again.

If anyone finds that he can't touch his heart sufficiently by this gentle correction, he can make use of a harsher, sharper rebuke in order to provoke himself. But after using severity and reproach, he still should end his anger and indignation with a calm, holy confidence in God....

When your heart has fallen, then, raise it gently, humbling yourself greatly before God, and acknowledging your fault. But don't wonder that you should fall. After all, it's no wonder that infirmity should be infirm, weakness weak, and frailty frail. Nevertheless, heartily detest the offense of which you have been guilty in God's sight, and with hearty courage and confidence in his mercy, begin once more to seek that virtue from which you have fallen away.

Introduction to the Devout Life

One day a hunter making his way through the brush came upon the abbot St. Anthony of the Desert relaxing and having a good time with his brother monks. The hunter was scandalized that a man with such a reputation for holiness should engage in activities other than rigorous spiritual disciplines. So St. Anthony wanted to teach him that we must make allowances for our weaknesses and humbly recognize our limits.

"Place an arrow in your bow," said the abbot to the hunter, "and draw it." He did so. "Draw it farther," said St. Anthony; and the hunter drew it farther. "Draw it yet farther," he insisted.

The hunter obeyed him, but he protested: "If I draw the bow too far, it will snap."

"So it is with doing God's work," answered the wise old abbot. "If we press ourselves excessively, we become exhausted. Sometimes it's best not to be rigid."

When the hunter heard these words, he repented of his previous thoughts, and the change of heart profited him greatly. For their part, the monks went home strengthened by the abbot's insight.

Sayings of the Fathers

Scrupulosity

Ours is a culture not often given to scrupulosity—that is, the tendency to experience unfounded fears that there is sin in our lives where there is none, or that our venial sins are more serious than is truly the case. We and our contemporaries seem much more likely to excuse or minimize our sins than to be scrupulous.

Nevertheless, among Christians who are serious about the vocation to holiness, this threat to interior peace is never far away. The word "scruple" comes from the Latin term meaning "small sharp stone," and those who suffer from scrupulosity can easily appreciate the derivation. Scruples are like tiny, pointed rocks scattered in the bed of the soul, keeping us from ever enjoying spiritual rest.

Blessed Henry Suso (c. 1295-1365), a Swiss Dominican evangelist and mystic, describes vividly the loss of peace in the scrupulous conscience.

Scrupulous souls, forever tormented by doubts and anxiety, have hearts that are ill prepared to receive Jesus Christ. In place

of that peace which religion is meant to give, these souls make
their lives miserable, full of trouble and temptation. Scrupulous
people distress themselves in many ways; for, really, they believe
no one, and no counsel brings calm to their troubled souls.
They keep returning to their sins and doubts, and the more they
think of them the more they aggravate the trouble.

*In her piercing examination of spiritual and psychological
maladies, St. Teresa of Avila addresses this problem as well. She
diagnoses the disorder as a kind of false humility and prescribes a
refocus of our thinking.*

Now be also on your guard, daughters, against some types of
humility given by the devil in which great disquiet is felt about
the gravity of our sins. This disturbance can afflict in many ways,
even to the point of making one give up receiving Communion
and practicing private prayer. These things are given up because
the devil makes one feel unworthy. And when such persons
approach the Blessed Sacrament, the time they used to spend in
receiving favors is now spent in wondering whether or not they
are well prepared. The situation gets so bad that the soul thinks
God has abandoned it because of what it is; it almost doubts his
mercy....

Sometimes it will be through humility and virtue that you hold
yourselves to be so wretched, and at other times it will be a gross
temptation.... [But] the pain of genuine humility doesn't agitate
or afflict the soul; rather, this humility expands it and enables it to
serve God more. The other type of pain disturbs everything, agi-
tates everything, afflicts the entire soul, and is very painful. I think
the devil's aim is to make us think we are humble and, in turn, if
possible, make us lose confidence in God.

When you find yourselves in this condition, stop thinking about your misery, insofar as possible, and turn your thoughts to the mercy of God, to how he loves us and suffered for us.

The Way of Perfection

St. Thomas More (1478-1535), an English statesman who was imprisoned in the Tower of London for his loyalty to the Church, agonized over the course he'd taken in opposing the ecclesiastical schism engineered by his friend and monarch, King Henry VIII. In the silence of his cell, the prisoner scrutinized his own motivations carefully; yet even as he faced his martyrdom, he never grew scrupulous, maintaining his sense of humor and his confidence that in the end God's grace would triumph.

The scrupulous person creates for himself many more fears than there is good cause to have, and many times a great fear where there is no cause for fear at all. What is no sin at all, he thinks to be a venial sin. And what is venial, he imagines to be mortal sin—and yet, despite his fears, he falls into these sins, since they are the kind that no man can be free of in this life for long.

Next he fears that he has never made a full confession or been fully contrite, and then that his sins are never fully forgiven him. So he goes to confession again and again, burdening his confessor as well as himself. Then with every prayer that he says, even though he may say it as well as the frail infirmity of man will allow, he fails to be satisfied unless he says the prayer again, and after that once more. And when he has prayed the same prayer three times, he is as little satisfied with the last time as he was with the first. So his heart always sinks in heaviness, agitation, and fear, full of doubt and dullness, without comfort or spiritual consolation.

With this dark fear the devil deeply troubles the mind of many a good man in order to bring him to some greater evil. For he can, if he wants to, drive such a man to such a fearful dread of God's rigorous justice that he will keep him from the comforting remembrance of God's great, mighty mercy. Thus he will make the scrupulous man do all his good works without consolation or liveliness. Worse yet, he makes him perceive as a sin something that isn't, and as a mortal sin one that's only venial....

Yes, and furthermore the devil longs to make all that man's good works and spiritual exercises so painful and so tedious to him that, with some other subtle suggestion or false, wily doctrine of a false spiritual liberty, he'll easily slide from that evil fault into one much worse—for the sake of the false ease and pleasure that he would suddenly find there. In this way he would have stretched his conscience as wide and large as it had been narrow and straight before....

Let those, then, who are in the troublesome fear of their own scrupulous conscience, submit the rule of their conscience to the counsel of some other good man. Such a counselor may shape his advice according to the nature and the variety of the man's scruples.

Yes, although a man may be very learned himself, yet if he is in this state, let him learn the custom among physicians. No matter how well trained one of them may be, when he himself is sick or diseased, he doesn't trust his care all to himself. Instead, he sends for those of his colleagues whom he knows to be competent and puts himself in their hands. He does this for many reasons, one of which is fear. For he may feel a great deal more fear than is necessary in response to certain symptoms, and at that point it would be better for his health if for the time being he didn't know about those symptoms....

Therefore I say, whoever has such a troublesome scrupulous conscience, let him for awhile refrain from judging himself, and follow the counsel of some other man whom he knows to be learned and virtuous—especially in the confessional. For there God is specially present with his grace assisting his sacrament. And he must not doubt that he should quiet his mind and follow what he's instructed to do there. He should think for a while less on the fear of God's justice, and be more merry in remembering his mercy. He should persevere in prayer for grace, abiding and dwelling faithfully in the sure hope of his help.

Then he shall find, without any doubt, that the shield of God's truth ... will surround him in such a way that he will not dread this dark fear of scrupulosity, but will afterward have his conscience established in good quiet and rest.

Dialogue of Comfort Against Tribulation

Despair

Despair is a sin against the virtue of hope, a giving up of our confidence that God desires and actively seeks our salvation. Though it sometimes seems to stem from excessive humility—"How could the Lord save a wretch like me?"—in truth, such humility is false, a deceiving mask worn by the kind of pride that makes the claim, if only implicitly, "I have the ability to commit sin so great that even God Almighty can't forgive it."

St. Augustine exhorts us to trust in God's mercy. To spur us on to hope, he paints a tragic portrait of the person who gives in to despair.

It is plain then, my brethren, it is plain to everyone—hold fast to it, be sure of it—that whenever anyone turns himself to faith in our Lord Jesus Christ, from a useless or abandoned way of life, all that is past is forgiven him. All his debts are canceled; a new account has been set up for him. Everything is entirely forgiven. So no one should be worried by the thought that there might remain anything that hasn't been forgiven him....

Consider how despair deceives us. Some people, when they begin to reflect on the evils they have done, conclude that they can't be forgiven. And once they conclude that, right away they give up their souls to ruin, perishing through despair.

They say to themselves: "Now there's no hope for people like me; sins as great as those we've committed can't be forgiven. So why not just satisfy our lusts? Let's at least grab all the pleasures of this life while we can, since we'll have no reward in the next life. Let's do whatever we want, even if it's not lawful—then, at least, we'll have a little fleeting pleasure, since we won't enjoy eternity."

In saying such things they lose their souls through despair, either before they ever come to believe at all, or when they're Christians already. They fall into evil living through many sins and acts of wickedness.

Nevertheless, the Lord of the vineyard goes out to them, and through the words of the prophet Ezekiel knocks on the door and calls to them in their despair. Even as they're turning their backs on him, he calls them: "On the day that a man shall turn from his wicked ways, I will forget all his iniquities" [see Ez 18:21]. If they hear and believe this voice, they will recover from despair, and rise up again from that deep, bottomless gulf in which they had been sunk.

Homilies on New Testament Lessons

The Sayings of the Fathers *is an ancient collection of wise observations and anecdotes compiled as an aid in living the Christian life, gathered from the saints of the desert monasteries in the early centuries of the Church. One story illustrates well St. Augustine's remarks about the potentially devastating consequences of despair.*

A young monk, we're told, was plagued for nine years by disturbing thoughts. Finally, he despaired of his salvation. Passing judgment on himself, he said: "My soul is ruined. Since I'm already damned, I'll go back to the world to live a life of sin."

On his way to the city, however, a Voice came to him, saying: "Those temptations you endured for nine years have become your crowns. Go back home, and I will take away your disturbing thoughts."

At that, the monk realized that we must not despair of ourselves because of temptations that come. If we make good use of temptations, they will become for us crowns.

If we would walk humbly with God, then despair isn't even an option, says Venerable Charles de Foucauld (1858-1916), a French priest, desert hermit, and African explorer who converted to the faith only after a youth of arrogant agnosticism and dissolution. Despite his struggles with sin, he recognized that holding on to hope was actually a matter of obedience to God. "However wicked I may be," *he once prayed,* "however great a sinner, I *must* hope that I will go to heaven. You forbid me to despair."

III.
PEACE WITH OTHERS

Since Christ says, "By this shall all men know that you are my disciples, if you love one another"; and since the Lord left his own peace to his disciples as a farewell gift, when about to complete his time on earth, saying, "Peace I leave with you, my peace I give you"; I cannot persuade myself that without love to others, and without, as far as rests with me, peace with everyone, I can be called a worthy servant of Jesus Christ.

St. Basil
Epistles

SEVEN

"CALLED TO PEACE"
So Many Good Reasons to Forgive

Put on then, as God's chosen ones, holy and beloved, compassion, kindness, lowliness, meekness, and patience, forbearing one another and, if one has a complaint against another, forgiving each other; as the Lord has forgiven you, so you also must forgive.... And let the peace of Christ rule in your hearts, to which indeed you were called in the one body.

St. Paul
COLOSSIANS 3:12-13, 15

Pardon one another so that later on you will not remember the injury. The recollection of an injury is in itself wrong. It adds to our anger, nurtures our sin, and hates what is good. It is a rusty arrow and poison for the soul. It puts all virtue to flight.

St. Francis de Paola (c. 1416-1507)

In the biblical book of Genesis, the tragic account of Adam and Eve's rebellion against God is followed immediately by the record of Cain's murder of Abel (see Genesis chapters 3 and 4). So it should. The two episodes, after all, form a single story: From the root of our revolt against heaven grows the bitter fruit of our conflict with one another.

No peace with God, then, means no peace with ourselves and no peace with others. Yet once our relationship with God has been restored, our gracious Lord has provided a way to restore our relationships with others as well. Just as forgiveness is the key to a renewed friendship with our Father in heaven, it's the key also to reconciliation with our brothers and sisters on earth.

Even so, for most of us, asking for and granting forgiveness is no easy task. When we suffer injuries, our anger clamors for justice rather than mercy. When we inflict injuries, our pride keeps us from admitting the wrong. Indignation ripens into bitterness, and bitterness, when long fermented, turns into hatred.

The saints have struggled like the rest of us with the challenge of forgiveness, gaining valuable insights into the dynamics of reconciliation. To those who, for whatever reasons, find themselves reluctant, they offer a number of persuasive reasons why we should forgive.

Why Forgive?

The three most important reasons to forgive stem from the most basic of Christian imperatives: obey God; recognize your own sins; and imitate Christ.

St. John Chrysostom reminds us of the most fundamental reason that we should forgive others: God Almighty, the King of the universe, has commanded us to do so.

What allowance then can be made for us, if even when we might receive so great a reward we still do not obey the Lawgiver's command to forgive one another, but rather persist in our contempt for him—for it's clear that, if we disobey, we're showing him contempt. Consider: If the Emperor had laid down a law, that all those who were enemies should be reconciled to one another, or else have their heads cut off, wouldn't everyone make haste to a reconciliation with his neighbor? Yes—truly, I think so! What excuse, then, do we have in not ascribing the same honor to the Lord that we would show to the Emperor, who is only our fellow servant?

Homilies on the Statues

St. Daniel (fourth century?), abbot of an ancient desert monastic community, recalls a true story about a brother monk that reveals the spiritual power unleashed by our obedience to God.

A nobleman's daughter in Babylon was once demon-possessed. When a monk came into her home one day to sell some of his handmade baskets, the demon agitated the girl to go up to him and slap him. Following Jesus' commandment, the monk turned to her his other cheek.

At that demonstration of meekness, the demon screamed through her, "Violence! The commandment of Jesus Christ is driving me out!" The devil was forced to leave, and the girl was instantly healed.

When they told the elder monks what had happened, they glorified God, declaring: "The pride of demons must fall before humble obedience to the commandments of Jesus Christ."

Sayings of the Fathers

St. Augustine emphasizes the lesson of Jesus' parable about the unmerciful servant: If God has forgiven us our debts, which are much greater than the debts owed to us by others, how dare we refuse to forgive others?

Peter asked his Master how often he should forgive a brother who had sinned against him, wondering whether seven times would be enough. The Lord answered him, "Not only seven times, but seventy times seven" [see Mt 18:22].

Then he added a parable that should terrify us, the story of the unmerciful servant who was forgiven a great debt by his master, but who then refused to forgive a much smaller debt owed him by his fellow servant [see vv. 23-35].... The king summoned that servant into his presence, and said to him, "You wicked servant! When you owed me so great a debt, in pity I forgave it all. Why then didn't you have compassion on your fellow servant, just as I had pity on you?" And he commanded that all the debt he'd forgiven the servant should be paid after all.

It is then for our instruction that Jesus presented this parable, and by this warning he wants to save us from perishing. "So," he said, "will my heavenly Father do to you as well, if from your hearts you fail to forgive every one of your brothers' offenses."

Well, brothers, the matter is plain and the admonition is useful.... For every man, at the same time, both is God's debtor and has also some brother who is a debtor to himself. For who can be found who isn't God's debtor, except for the one who has no sin? And who is there who has no one else as his debtor, except someone against whom no one has ever sinned? Do you think that anyone on earth can be found, who isn't himself bound to his brother by some sin? So then everyone is a debtor, and everyone has his own debtors, too.

For that reason, a just God appoints a rule for you to observe with regard to your debtor—the same rule he will observe with his debtors.... Would you be forgiven? Then forgive.

Homilies on New Testament Lessons

St. Cyprian of Carthage, writing to his flock On the Advantage of Patience, *points out that Christ forgave his enemies, and he is our model, to be imitated in all things.*

In his very passion and cross, even before they had gone as far as accomplishing the cruelty of death and the spilling of blood, what infamies of reproach he patiently heard, what mockings of contempt he suffered! He who with his spittle had a little while before made a blind man to see, was spit upon by those who insulted him. He in whose name the devil and his angels are now scourged by his servants, suffered scourgings himself!

He who crowns martyrs with eternal flowers was crowned with thorns.... He who clothes others in the raiment of immortality was stripped of his earthly clothes. He who gave heavenly food was fed with gall. He who served the cup of salvation was given vinegar to drink.

That guiltless, that righteous One—he who is himself innocence and justice—was counted among transgressors. He who is truth was oppressed with false witnesses. He who will judge was judged; and the Word of God was led silently to the slaughter.

Then, when at the cross of the Lord the stars are confounded, the elements are disturbed, the earth quakes, night shuts out the day, the sun—so that he may not be compelled to look on the crime—withdraws his light and covers his face, even then Christ doesn't speak, nor is he undone, nor does he declare his majesty; no, not even in his terrible passion. Even to the end, he bears all things with perseverance and constancy, in order that in him a full and perfect patience may be fulfilled. And after all these things, Christ still welcomes his murderers, if they will be converted and come to him. With a saving patience, he who is gracious to preserve us from perishing closes his Church to no one. Those adversaries, those blasphemers, those who were always enemies to his name, if they repent of their sin, if they acknowledge the crime committed, he receives—not only to pardon their sin, but to grant them the reward of the heavenly kingdom. What could be more patient, what more merciful? Even the one who has shed Christ's blood is made alive by Christ's blood....

But if we also, beloved brethren, are in Christ; if we put him on, if he is the way of our salvation for those who follow Christ in the footsteps of salvation, then we must walk according to Christ's example, as the apostle John instructs us: "He who says he abides in Christ, ought himself to walk even as he walked" [see 1 Jn 2:6]. Peter also, on whom by the Lord's condescension the Church was founded, lays it down in his epistle, and says: "Christ suffered for us, leaving you an example, that you should follow in his steps, who committed no sin, nor was deceit found in his mouth; who, when he was reviled, did not revile in return; when He suffered, he did not threaten, but entrusted himself to the One who judges justly" [see 1 Pt 2:21-23].

What We Gain When We Forgive

After urging us to follow those three basic Christian principles, the saints advise us that forgiving one another yields a wide range of good spiritual fruit. "Peace," notes St. Francis de Sales, "is better than a fortune." The hope of recovering such a valuable possession should be a strong incentive to forgiveness in itself. Yet there are a number of other precious goods obtained when we let go of offenses and seek reconcilation with others.

Becoming like God, St. John Cassian (360-435) told his brother monks, is the goal of the Christian life. And what could make us more like him than to be merciful as he is merciful?

Whoever then by practicing charity has attained the image and likeness of God will delight in goodness for the pleasure of goodness itself. Having a godly feeling of patience and gentleness, he will from then on be angered by no faults of sinners; rather, in his compassion and sympathy, he will ask for pardon for their infirmities. Remembering that for so long he himself was tested by the stings of similar passions, until by the Lord's mercy he was saved, he will feel that, as he was saved from carnal attacks not by his own exertions but by God's protection, not anger but pity ought to be shown to those who go astray....

And while he continues in this humility of mind he will even be able to fulfill this evangelical command of perfection: "Love your enemies, do good to those who hate you, and pray for those who persecute you and slander you" [see Lk 6:27-28]. And so it will be granted to us to attain that reward which is attached to this command: that we will not only bear the image and likeness of God, but will even be called his sons. Do this, Jesus says, "so that you may be sons of your Father who is in heaven, for he makes his sun rise on the evil and on the good, and sends rain on the just and on the unjust" [Lk 6:35; Mt 5:45].

This confidence the blessed John knew he had attained when he said: "that we may have confidence for the day of judgment, because as he is so are we in this world" [1 Jn 4:17]. For in what can a weak and fragile human nature be like him, except in always showing a calm love in its heart toward the good and evil, the just and the unjust, in imitation of God, and by doing good for the love of goodness itself, arriving at that true adoption of the sons of God?

Conferences

On a more practical level, St. John Cassian and Blessed Henry Suso point out that a conciliatory attitude can defuse our adversary's hostility toward us.

Evangelical perfection ... teaches that patience must be maintained, not in words but in inward tranquillity of heart, and bids us preserve it whatever evil happens. In this way, we may not only keep ourselves always from disturbing anger, but also—by submitting to their injuries—compel those who are disturbed by their own fault to become calm when they have had their fill of striking us. Thus we overcome their rage by our gentleness, fulfilling these words of the apostle: "Do not be overcome by evil, but overcome evil with good" [Rom 12:21].

St. John Cassian
Conferences

You shall die to yourself so utterly that you will not go to sleep at night until you have sought out your tormentor and, as far as possible, calmed his angry heart with your sweet words and ways. For with such meek lowliness you will take from him his sword and knife, and make him powerless in his ill will.

Blessed Henry Suso

Are you worried that if you forgive your offenders, they won't be motivated to repent of their wrongdoing? Leave that problem to God, says St. John Chrysostom. He can correct sinners more effectively than we can.

Has your neighbor wronged and offended you, and involved you in a thousand troubles? Even if he has, don't seek revenge, or you might be showing contempt to your Lord! Yield the matter to God, and he will dispose of it much better than you could even hope for.

To you the Lord has given instructions simply to pray for the offender. How to deal with the offender, God has commanded you to leave to himself. Never could you avenge yourself as he is prepared to avenge you, if you give him room to do it, not cursing the one who has offended you, but rather allowing God to be the sole arbiter of the sentence.

For although we may pardon those who have injured us; although we may be reconciled; although we may pray for them; yet God does not pardon them, unless they themselves are converted to him and repent. And he withholds his pardon for their own benefit. While God praises you and commends you for your spiritual wisdom in forgiving, he doesn't want the offender to grow worse because he escaped correction through your patience. God will deal with him.

Homilies on the Statues

Why "turn the other cheek"? St. Anthony Zaccaria (1502-39), founder of the Clerks Regular of St. Paul, devoted his life to works of mercy joined to effective preaching. When his comrades encountered hostility and opposition to their work, he reminded them: Good is stronger than evil; forgiving others may contribute to their conversion.

We should pray for [our enemies] and and not be overcome by evil, but overcome evil by goodness. We should heap good works like red-hot coals of burning love upon their heads, as our apostle urges us to do [see Rom 12:20]. So that when they become aware of our tolerance and gentleness they may undergo a change of heart and be prompted to turn in love to God.

The Daily Office

Forgiving those who injure us, notes St. Augustine, may also contribute to their conversion, because our willingness to lose earthly goods for the sake of heavenly ones provides them with an object lesson about what kind of wealth is truly worth pursuing.

But who, even if he's a stranger to our religion, is so deaf as not to know how many precepts enjoining peace ... are continually read in the churches of Christ? For this is the intent of those precepts: That to the one who strikes us on one cheek we should offer the other to be struck; to the one who would take away our coat we should give our cloak as well; and that with the one who compels us to go one mile we should go two [see Mt 5:39-41].

These things are to be done so that a wicked man may be overcome by kindness, or rather that the evil in the wicked man may be overcome by good, and that the man may be delivered from that evil.... For this reason, the one who is overcoming evil by good submits patiently to the loss of merely earthly advantages. The offender's excessive love for such worldly things is what made him wicked in the first place; so when the person injured gives them up, he shows how such things are of little worth in comparison to faith and righteousness. In this way, the offender may learn from the person he wronged what is the true nature of the things for the sake of which he committed the wrong, and may be won back to peace with sorrow for his sin....

Thus the offender will be overcome, not by the strength of

someone's passionate resentment, but by the good nature of someone patiently bearing wrong. Turning the other cheek has its intended effect, then, when it seems that it will benefit the one for whose sake it is done, by producing in him a change in his ways and peace with others. At all events, it is to be done with this intention—even though the result may be different from what was expected, and the man whose correction and reconciliation was to be accomplished through this healing "medicine" refuses to be corrected and reconciled.

Epistles

Those who are patient and forgiving are often accused of weakness. No, replies St. John Cassian: the exercise of patience and forgiveness actually develops spiritual strength and demonstrates spiritual stamina.

The nature of the weak is always such that they are quick and ready to offer reproaches and sow the seeds of quarrels, while they themselves can't bear to be touched by the shadow of the very slightest wrong. While they are riding roughshod over us and flinging about wanton charges, they aren't able to bear even the slightest and most trivial ones themselves....

But you must certainly know that in general he plays a stronger part who subjects his own will to his brother's, than he who is found to be the more obstinate, defending and clinging to his own decisions. For the former by bearing and putting up with his neighbor gains a strong and vigorous character, while the latter gains a weak and sickly one....

For this is the apostle's command: "We who are strong ought to bear with the failings of the weak" [Rom 15:1]; and "Bear one another's burdens, and so fulfill the law of Christ" [Gal 6:2]. For a weak man will never support a weak man, nor can one who is suffering in the same way bear or cure one in feeble health. Rather, someone who is himself not subject to infirmity brings remedies to the one in weak health.

Conferences

There is one final, powerful incentive to be merciful. If you have sins to be forgiven—and who doesn't?—then remember this, says St. John Chrysostom: Forgiving others secures forgiveness of your own sins by God.

Haven't you heard about the servant in the parable who owed the ten thousand talents and then, after he was forgiven that debt, seized his fellow servant by the throat for the sake of a few pennies? What great evils he underwent, delivered over to an endless punishment! Don't you tremble at his example? Have you no fear of suffering the same fate?

For we too owe to our Lord many great debts. Nevertheless, he is patient and long-suffering; he doesn't press us, as we do our fellow servants, nor does he choke us and take us by the throat. Yet certainly, had he decided to exact of us even the least part of what we owe him, we would have perished long ago.

So, beloved, bearing these things in mind, we must be humbled and feel thankful to those who are in debt to us. For they become to us, if we control ourselves, an occasion of obtaining abundant pardon; and giving a little, we will receive much. Why then demand the trifle from those indebted to us, when we could forgive that debt and receive in return a cancellation of our entire debt to God?

But if you're violent and contentious, you'll have none of your own debts forgiven. While you think you're hurting your neighbor, you're actually thrusting the sword into yourself, increasing your punishment in hell. But if you will show a little self-control here, you'll take care of your own accounts with God. For in fact God wants us to take the lead in that kind of generosity, so that he can take the occasion to repay us with interest.

As many, then, as stand indebted to you, either for money or for injuries, let them all go free, and ask God for the reward of such generosity. For as long as they continue to be indebted to you, you can't have God as your debtor. But if you let them go free, you will be able to detain your God and require of him a bountiful reward for such great self-restraint.

Homilies on the Gospel of St. Matthew

EIGHT

"A FORETASTE OF HELL"
Perils of Failing to Forgive

Then in anger his master handed him over to the torturers until he should pay back the whole debt. So will my heavenly Father do to you, unless each of you forgives his brother from his heart.

MATTHEW 18:34-35, NAB

There is no sin nor wrong that gives a man such a foretaste of hell in this life as anger and impatience.

St. Catherine of Siena (1347-80)
Letter to Mona Agnese

Caught in the raucous arena of national politics, St. Thomas More was no stranger to the deadly consequences of bitterness. As Lord Chancellor of England, he had witnessed the rise and fall of ambitious men as they played their ruthless games of deceit and manipulation, insincere alliance and easy betrayal, clawing and climbing over one another in their quest for power and status. For many such politicians, no doubt, anger was a way of life, and the thought of forgiving a political enemy was laughable.

The resulting sickness of the soul, St. Thomas observed, was a "deadly cancer ... from which so much harm grows: It makes us unlike ourselves, makes us like timber wolves or furies from hell, drives us forth headlong upon the points of swords, makes us blindly run forth after other men's destruction as we hasten toward our own ruin."

Reasons to Avoid Bitterness

Such sobering remarks are confirmed by the consensus of the saints. If the positive goods obtained by pardoning others don't provide us sufficient incentive to forgive, then we need only listen to the warnings of the saints: Failure to forgive, they agree, leads to disaster. The many fruits of bitterness are more costly than we can afford.

If we don't forgive others, St. Augustine soberly warns us, we're in no position to ask God to forgive us. What could be worse?

What a grave temptation in this life it is, dearly beloved, when the matter about which we're tempted is the very issue that will decide whether we're forgiven for succumbing to any other temptation. What a frightful test it is that, if failed, could cause us to lose our ability to recover from the failure of any other test....

What then is that horrifying temptation, that most serious, that tremendous temptation, which must be avoided with all our strength, with all our resolution? The temptation to avenge ourselves. Anger is kindled, and you burn to be avenged. What a frightful temptation! By giving in to it, you're losing what's necessary to receive forgiveness for all your other faults.

If you had committed a sin of some other kind, if you had

given in to some other lust, you could have found a cure in God's forgiveness, because you could have prayed, "Forgive us our debts, as we also forgive our debtors." But whoever provokes you to take vengeance will steal from you the ability to say, "As we also forgive our debtors." When that ability is lost, all sins are retained; nothing at all is remitted....

This is what we must always be saying: "Forgive us our debts." What debts? There is no lack of them, for we are only human. Perhaps I have talked somewhat too much, said something I shouldn't have said, laughed when I shouldn't have, eaten more than I should have, listened with pleasure to something I shouldn't have, drunk more than I should have, looked with pleasure on something I shouldn't have, thought with pleasure on something I shouldn't have.

"Forgive us our debts, as we also forgive our debtors." If you have lost this prayer, you yourself are lost.

Homilies on New Testament Lessons

Failure to Forgive Separates Us From God

Do you want to be close to God? Then you'd better practice forgiveness, insist the saints. Our failure to forgive angers him and separates us from him. St. Agatho (d. 681) sums up the matter pointedly: "If an angry man raises the dead," he observes, "God is still displeased with his anger."

St. Ephraim (306?-c. 373), a deacon of Syria whose celebrated hymns earned him the nickname "harp of the Holy Spirit," reasons that to be alienated from a fellow human being, who is God's image, is to be alienated from God himself.

If you're angry at your neighbor, you're angry at God; and if you carry bitterness in your heart, you've boldly lifted yourself up against your Lord.... So if you love to be angry, be angry with wickedness, and that should suit you well; if you want to wage war, fight Satan, your true adversary; if you want to insult someone, curse the demons.

Consider: According to the law, if you were to insult the king's image, you would pay the same penalty as murder. Well, if you insult a human being, you're insulting the image of God! Honor your neighbor, and you have honored God. But if you want to dishonor him, accuse your neighbor angrily!...

The sign that you love God is this: that you love your fellow men. But if you hate your fellow men, your hatred is toward God.... For the soul is the image of the Creator, so honor the image of God by being at peace with all men....

You've been bought with the blood of God; you're redeemed by the passion of Christ; for your sake he suffered death, so that you might die to your sins. His face endured spitting so that you might not shrink from scorn. He drank vinegar and gall so that you might lay anger aside....

If you are his true disciple, walk in your Master's footsteps. Endure scorn from your brother so that you may be the companion of Christ. Don't show anger against men so that you may not be separated from your Redeemer.

On Admonition and Repentance

Jesus said: "If you are offering your gift at the altar, and there remember that your brother has something against you, leave your gift there before the altar and go; first be reconciled to your brother, and then come and offer your gift" (Mt 5:23-24). When we go to the altar in disobedience to this command of our Lord, say St. Augustine and St. John Chrysostom, we're subject to God's judgment.

How many receive at the altar and die—indeed, who die by receiving? That's why the apostle says that it's possible for someone who eats and drinks the Lord's Body and Blood to "eat and drink judgment upon himself" [see 1 Cor 11:29]. For the morsel given by the Lord to Judas wasn't poison; and yet when he took it, the enemy entered into him—not because he received an evil thing, but because he, being evil, received a good thing in an evil way.

See to it, then, brothers, that you eat the heavenly bread in a spiritual sense by bringing innocence to the altar. Though your sins may be daily, at least don't let them be deadly. Before you approach the altar, consider well what you will be praying: "Forgive us our debts, even as we forgive our debtors."

If you forgive, it will be forgiven you: approach in peace; it is bread, not poison. But make sure you have forgiven; for if you don't, you're lying, and you're lying to the One you can't deceive. You can lie to God, but you can't deceive him. He knows what you're doing. He sees you within, examines you within, inspects you within, judges you within—and within he either condemns or crowns.

St. Augustine
Homilies on the Gospel of St. John

God's law bids us consider no man as an enemy, nor retain resentment long, but to be reconciled right away.... And just as it is not to be imagined that the fornicator and the blasphemer can partake of the sacred Table, so it is impossible that someone who has an enemy, and bears malice, can enjoy the Holy Communion. And this with good reason.

For a man, when he has committed fornication or adultery, once he has satisfied his lust, has also completed the sin. Should he be willing by careful living to recover from that fall, he may afterward, by manifesting great penitence, obtain some relief. But whoever is resentful works the same iniquity every day, and never brings it to an end. In the former case the deed is over, and the sin completed; but here the sin is perpetrated every day.

What excuse can we have, I ask then, for delivering ourselves willingly to such an evil monster? How can you ask your Lord to be mild and merciful to you, when you have been so hard and unforgiving to your fellow servant?

St. John Chrysostom
Homilies on the Statues

"Anything you may do to avenge yourself upon a brother who has done you an injustice will cause you to stumble during prayer," *notes St. Nilus of Sinai (d. c. 340), an abbot of ancient Egypt. St. John Cassian elaborates further on how failure to forgive hinders our prayers.*

Whatever our mind has been thinking of before the hour of prayer is sure to occur to us while we're praying through the activity of the memory. For that reason, whatever we want to find ourselves like while we're praying, that's what we ought to prepare ourselves to be before the time for prayer. For the mind in prayer is formed by its previous condition, and when we're applying ourselves to prayer, the images of the same actions and words and thoughts will dance before our eyes and make us angry, as in our previous condition....

So if we don't want anything to haunt us while we're praying, we should be careful before our prayer to exclude that thing from the shrine of our heart, so that we may in this way fulfill the apostle's injunction: ... "I desire then that in every place the men should pray, lifting holy hands without anger or quarreling" [see 1 Tm 2:8].

Conferences

Yet bitterness is more than just a distraction when we pray, says St. Ephraim. To pray while we harbor resentment in our hearts is an insult to God.

For it is blasphemy if you stand before God praying while you're angry. For even your own heart convicts you then that you're piling up your words in vain. Your conscience rightly judges that your prayers are profiting you nothing.

Christ as he hung high on the tree interceded for his murderers—yet you who are dust, a son of the clay, are filled with rage. You remain angry with your brother, and still you dare to pray? Watch out!... Let go of your rage and then pray— unless you want to provoke God even further. Restrain your anger, and then you can make your requests to God.

On Admonition and Repentance

Hindered Spiritual Growth

Not just our prayers, but our spiritual growth as a whole is hindered by our failure to forgive, say Pope St. Gregory the Great (540-604) and St. John Chrysostom. Bitterness is a root that bears a variety of poisonous spiritual fruit.

For those who are quarreling are to be admonished to know most certainly that, in whatever virtues they may abound, they can by no means become spiritual if they neglect becoming united to their neighbors in peace. For it is written, "But the fruit of the Spirit is love, joy, peace" [Gal 5:22]. So whoever has no desire to keep peace refuses to bear the fruit of the Spirit. That's why Paul says, "For while there is jealousy and strife among you, are you not of the flesh?" [1 Cor 3:3].

Again, he says, "Strive for peace with all men, and for the holiness without which no one will see the Lord" [Heb 12:14]. Then he admonishes once more, saying, "[Be] eager to maintain the unity of the Spirit in the bond of peace. There is one body and one Spirit, just as you were called in one hope of your calling" [see Eph 4:3-4]. The one hope of our calling, therefore, is never reached if we don't run to it with a mind at one with our neighbors.

Pope St. Gregory the Great
The Book of Pastoral Rule

Nothing so fills the mind with impurity as anger that remains constantly within it. The Spirit of meekness will not settle where wrath or passion dwell; and when a man is destitute of the Holy Spirit, what hope of salvation can he have, and how will he walk aright? So beloved, don't cast yourself down headfirst by seeking revenge on your enemy; don't cause yourself to be left alone without the protection of God!

St. John Chrysostom
Homilies on the Statues

"If a monk should grow angry," *St. Macarius (300-390) observes,* "unless he is quickly protected by humbling himself, in a short time—troubled as he is, and troubling others—he comes under the power of the devil." *St. Ephraim agrees: Just as reconciliation draws us closer to God, he claims, dissension draws us closer to Satan.*

Whenever you strive with your brother, Satan abides in peace. Whenever you envy your fellow man, you give rest to demons. Whenever you talk about the shortcoming of those who aren't present, your tongue has made a harp for the music of the devil. Whenever hatred is in your soul, great is the peace of the deceiver.

On Admonition and Repentance

Are you counting on spiritual exercises to help you grow in holiness? They are of little value, warns the ancient African abbot St. Moses (c. 330-c. 445), if you're filled with anger.

Perfection isn't arrived at simply by self-denial ... unless there is that charity ... which consists in purity of heart alone. For not to be envious, not to be puffed up, not to be angry, not to seek one's own way, not to take pleasure in wrongdoing, not to think evil [see 1 Cor 13:4-6]—what is all this except to offer to God always a perfect and clean heart, and to keep it free from all disturbances?

Everything should be done and sought after by us for the sake of this goal. For this we must seek for solitude, for this we know that we ought to submit to fasting, vigils, toils, bodily nakedness, spiritual reading, and all other virtues, so that through them we may be enabled to prepare our heart and to keep it unharmed by all evil passions. Then, resting on these steps of the spiritual disciplines, we can mount to the perfection of charity.

With regard to all these disciplines, if by accident we've been preoccupied in some good and useful activity and have been unable to carry out our customary discipline, then we should not be overcome by vexation, anger, or other passions. For it was the very object of overcoming such passions in the first place that led us to undertake those disciplines. The spiritual benefits we gain from fasting won't make up for the losses we incur through anger, nor is the profit from spiritual reading so great as the harm that results from despising a brother.

Quoted in St. John Cassian, *Conferences*

Pope St. Leo the Great urged his flock to remember during Lent that abstention from foods means nothing if we don't abstain from resentment as well.

For our Lenten fast does not consist chiefly of mere abstinence from food, nor are delicacies withdrawn from our bodily appetites with profit, unless the mind is recalled from wrongdoing and the tongue restrained from slandering. This is a time of gentleness and long-suffering, of peace and tranquility—when all the pollutions of vice are to be eradicated and steadfastness of virtue is to be attained by us.

Now let godly minds boldly accustom themselves to forgive faults, to pass over insults, and to forget wrongs. Now let the faithful spirit train himself with the armor of righteousness on the right hand and on the left, so that through honor and dishonor, through ill repute and good repute, the conscience may be undisturbed in unwavering uprightness, not puffed up by the praise of others nor wearied by their insults.

Sermons

St. Albert the Great (c. 1206-80) lived in a time when great throngs set out each spring to make long pilgrimages as a form of penance. This wise professor and philosopher at the University of Paris, who mentored the great theologian St. Thomas Aquinas, reminded his fellow scholars: "To forgive those who have injured us in our body, our reputations, our goods, will profit us more than to go on pilgrimage across the sea to venerate the sepulchre of the Lord."

Bitterness Leads to Blindness

A striking theme runs throughout the observations of the saints on the effects of failing to forgive: Bitterness is a form of blindness. St. John Cassian offers a scriptural basis for this truth; St. Thomas Aquinas adds a practical note about why anger clouds our vision of reality.

As long as anger remains in our hearts, and blinds with its hurtful darkness the eye of the soul, we can neither acquire right judgment and discretion, nor gain the insight that springs from an honest gaze, nor mature counsel. Nor can we be partakers of life, nor maintain righteousness, nor even have the capacity for spiritual and true light—"for," says the Scripture, "My eye is troubled through indignation" [Ps 6:8, Douay-Rheims]. Nor can we become partakers of wisdom, even though we are considered wise by universal consent, for "anger resteth in the bosom of a fool" [Eccl 7:9]. ...Nor shall we be able with clear judgment of heart to secure a steadfast righteousness, even though we may be reckoned perfect and holy in the estimation of all men, for "the anger of man does not work the righteousness of God" [Jas 1:20].

St. John Cassian
Institutes

Any disturbance of the body hinders the judgment of reason, as is clear in the case of drunkenness or sleep. Now anger, above all, causes a bodily disturbance in the region of the heart, so much so that it affects even the outward members of the body. Consequently, of all the passions, anger is the most manifest obstacle to the judgment of reason.

St. Thomas Aquinas
Summa Theologica

Bitterness not only blinds us; it isolates us. St. Basil (329-79), one of the great Eastern theologians of the early Church, was archbishop of Caesaria; he once wrote a letter to admonish a younger bishop about the dangerous consequences of holding a grudge.

If I continue to insist on the privileges to which my superior age entitles me and wait for you to take the initiative in communication; and if you, my friend, wish to adhere more persistently to your misguided strategy of inaction; when will our silence ever come to an end? However, where friendship is involved, to be defeated is in my opinion to win, and so I am quite ready to give you precedence, and retire from the contest over which of us should insist on being right. I have been the first to take up a pen, because I know that "love bears all things ... endures all things ... does not insist on its own way" and thus "never fails" [see 1 Cor 13:5-8]. Whoever submits himself to his neighbor in love can never be humiliated.

I do beg you, then, at all events for the future, show the first and greatest fruit of the Spirit: love. Away with the angry man's sullenness you are showing me by your silence, and recover joy in your heart, peace with the brothers who are of one mind with you, and zeal and anxiety for the continued safety of the churches of the Lord....

I exhort you then, drive out of your mind the idea that you need communion with no one else. To cut one's self off from connection with the brethren is not the mark of one who is walking by love, nor yet the fulfilling of the commandment of Christ.

Epistle to Bishop Atarbius

In these and other ways, the saints agree, bitterness devastates and destroys the soul. St. Simeon the New Theologian (949-1022), a medieval Byzantine mystic and spiritual writer, speaks of bitterness as the venom of that ancient serpent, the devil.

A man who is deeply wounded in his heart by provocation and abuse shows that deep in himself he harbors the old serpent. If he bears the blows in silence and answers with great humility, he will render this serpent weak and powerless, or will kill it altogether. But if he argues with bitterness or speaks with arrogance, he will give the serpent an added strength to pour poison into his heart and mercilessly to devour his entrails.

Philokalia

Rage is a disorder, says St. John Chrysostom. It damages the soul in the same way that a chemical imbalance damages our bodies.

Nothing is more injurious to us than rage and fierce anger.... For consider how it is with our bodies: Disorders arise from excess. When the chemicals of our bodies become unbalanced, and certain substances are increased to abnormal levels, the result is that countless diseases are generated, leading to painful kinds of death. A similar situation arises in the soul as well.

Homilies on the Gospel of St. Matthew

114 / The Saints' Guide to Making Peace with God, Yourself and Others

St. Cyprian of Carthage piles image upon image in his effort to convince us that bitterness is deadly: Think of it, he says, as spiritual thorns, thistles, poison, virus, infection. Get rid of it before it ruins you!

If you who were once possessed with jealousy and rancor want eternal rewards, cast away all that malice that has held you fast, and be reformed to the way of eternal life in the footsteps of salvation. Tear out from your breast thorns and thistles, so that the Lord's seed may enrich you with a fertile produce, and the divine and spiritual cornfield may abound to the plenty of a fruitful harvest. Cast out the poison of gall, cast out the virus of discords. Let the mind that the malice of the serpent once infected be purged; let all bitterness that had settled within be softened by the sweetness of Christ....

Your debts shall be forgiven you when you yourself shall have forgiven. Your sacrifices shall be received when you shall come before God in peace with others.

On Jealousy and Envy

NINE

"HATE THE DISEASE, NOT THE PATIENT"
Finding God's Perspective on Conflict

*Give up your anger, abandon your wrath; do not be provoked, it brings only harm. Those who do evil will be cut off....
wait a little, and the wicked will be no more.*

PSALM 37:8-10, NAB

Anger is a kind of temporary insanity.
St. Basil (329-379)

Anger, as we've seen, has deadly consequences. Perhaps even worse is its blurring of our spiritual vision. "The emotion of wrath boils over," observes St. John Cassian, "and blinds the eyes of the soul." Not surprisingly, reconciliation becomes all the more difficult when we fail to see clearly our adversaries or ourselves.

The remedy? God sees things as they truly are, so we do well to seek his perspective—which is, after all, simply another name for wisdom. If we try to take God's point of view into consideration, we'll find it easier to forgive and make peace.

Seeing As God Sees

The saints offer a number of insights to help us readjust our focus and recover our spiritual vision. Consider these:

God sees both you and your offender as sinners in need of forgiveness, says St. John Chrysostom. Keep your own sins in mind, and you'll find it easier to forgive; your fear of punishment will drive out your anger.

Your mind is inflamed by the memory of your enemy. It grows swollen, and your heart rises. Whenever the memory of the one who has caused you pain comes back to you, you're unable to keep your thoughts from swelling to fill your mind.

But set against this inflammation the memory of sins you yourself have committed, so that you begin to fear the resulting punishment to come. Recall how many things you're accountable for to your Master, and that for all those things you owe him satisfaction. The fear will surely overcome the anger, since it's certainly far more powerful than that passion.

Recall the memory of hell, punishment, and vengeance during the time of your prayer, and the thought of your enemy won't even be able to enter your mind. Make your mind contrite. Humble your soul by the memory of the offenses you've committed, and anger won't even be able to trouble you.

But the cause of all these evils is this: We scrutinize the sins of everyone else with great exactitude, while we negligently let our own sins pass by. Yet we ought to do the contrary—never to forget our own faults, but never even to admit a thought of the faults of others.

Homily Against Publicizing the Errors of the Brethren

A young monk came to the abbot St. Poemen (fourth century) complaining about the sins of another monk. Once the youth finished speaking, the old man wanted to remind him of his condition before God. So he looked down at the ground and picked up a wisp of straw.

"What is this?" he asked.

"Straw," answered the young monk.

Next the abbot reached up to touch the roof of his cell. "What is this?" he asked.

"The beam," said the other monk, "that holds up your roof."

"Take it into your heart," said St. Poemen, "that your sins are like this beam, and your brother's sins are like this wisp of straw."

Sayings of the Fathers

Do you try to make excuses for failing to forgive? In God's eyes, says St. John Chrysostom, you have no excuse.

For what is easier, I ask, than to get rid of resentment against the injurer? Is there any long journey to be undertaken? Is there any expenditure of money? Is the aid of others to be invoked? All we have to do is resolve to let go of the offense, and the good deed is done at once....

If I say, "Practice fasting," you may plead to be excused because of bodily weakness. If I say, "Give to the poor," you may say you're too poor, or that your money must go to the expenses of bringing up children. If I say, "Make time to go to church," you may say worldly cares prevent you. If I say, "Pay attention to what is spoken in the homily, and consider the power of the teaching," you may say you lack the education to understand it. If I say, "Correct another person," you may say, "When he gets advice, he pays no attention; I've often tried to help him, but he scoffed at me."

As frigid as such pretenses are, at least you still have some pretenses to use. But suppose I say, "Dismiss your anger." Which of these pretenses will you use then?" For neither physical infirmity, nor poverty, nor lack of culture, nor lack of time, nor any other thing of that kind can you offer as an excuse. Above all others, then, the sin of failing to forgive is the most inexcusable.

Homilies on the Statues

If you look at offenses against you the way God does, says St. Francis of Assisi (c. 1181-1226), you'll find that your grief over the state of the offender's soul overwhelms your anger.

The Lord says: "Love your enemies" [Mt 5:44]. That person truly loves his enemy who is not upset at any injury which is done to himself, but out of love of God is disturbed at the sin of the other's soul. And let him show his love for the other by his deeds.

The Admonitions

The fifth-century historian Sulpitius Severus describes how St. Martin of Tours (c. 316-97), the great missionary bishop of ancient Gaul, wept for his enemies.

No one ever saw [him] enraged.... Never was there any word on his lips but Christ, and never was there a feeling in his heart except piety, peace, and tender mercy. Frequently, too, he used to weep for the sins of those who insulted him—those who, as he led his retired and tranquil life, slandered him with poisoned tongue and a viper's mouth ... who were envious of his virtues and his life ... who really hated in him what they did not see in themselves, and despised what they lacked the power to imitate.

Life of St. Martin of Tours

How can we possibly love our enemies—people who may be wicked; people who wish us harm? Love them as God does, says St. Augustine: not for what they are, but for what you want them to become.

You do not love in your enemies what they are, but what you would have them to become. Suppose there is a log of timber lying around. A skilled carpenter sees the log, not yet planed, just as it was hewn in the forest. He takes a liking to it because he wants to make something out of it. He is not attracted to it for the purpose of leaving it as it is. In his craft he has seen what it will become, and his liking is for what he will make of it, not for what it is now.

In the same way we say that God loved sinners.... Did he love us sinners for the purpose of keeping us sinners? No—our Carpenter viewed us as unplaned logs, and he had in mind the building he would make of us, not the rough timber that we were....

As the Lord viewed you, you too must view your enemies, those who oppose you, raging, biting with words, frustrating you with their slander, harassing you with their hatred. You must remember that they are human beings; you must see all their actions against you as merely human works, while they themselves are the works of God. That your enemies have been created is God's doing; that they hate you and wish your ruin is their own doing.

What should you say about them in your mind? "Lord, be

merciful to them, forgive them their sins, put the fear of God in them, change them!" You are loving in them not what they are, but what you would have them to become.

Homilies on First John

You wouldn't want to have a saint for an enemy, would you? Of course not. So, love the one who has offended you, says the Spanish archbishop St. Thomas of Villanova (1488-1555). No doubt God has great plans for that person.

Dismiss all anger and look into yourself a little. Remember that he of whom you are speaking is your brother and, as he is walking along the way of salvation, God can make him a saint in spite of his present weakness.

Be like the Great Physician, St. Augustine reminds us: Hate the sickness; love the patient.

Do not be slow to love your enemies. Are there those who rage against you? If so, pray for them. Do they hate you? Pity them. It is actually the sick fever in their souls that hates you; one day they will be healed, and they will thank you.

Be like our physicians: How do they love those who are ill? Is it the illness itself that they love? If they loved their patients for being sick, they would want them always to be sick. But they love those who are ill, not so that they will remain that way, but so that their illness will be healed.

And how much does the doctor put up with when patients are delirious! What rude, foul language! Often such patients go so far as to strike the doctor. Yet the doctor attacks the fever while forgiving the patient.

What shall we say, brothers and sisters: Does the physician

love his enemy? No—he hates his enemy, because his enemy is the disease, not the patient.

Even if a delirious patient strikes him, he still loves the patient but hates the fever that causes the delirium. For who is it that really struck him? Not the patient, but the delirium, the fever, the illness itself.

So he works to get rid of the sickness that fights against him, so that the patient who survives will give him thanks. And so should you. If your enemies hate you, and hate you without cause, remember that the ungodly passions of the world control them like a fever, making them hate you.

Homilies on First John

St. Simeon the New Theologian tells us we should actually be grateful to those who injure us. After all, God often uses them as tools for refining us. "A man," *St. Simeon observes,* "who is well disposed toward and loves those who revile and abuse him and cause him harm, and who prays for them, in a short time attains to great achievements."

St. Thomas More experienced just such a refining at the hands of his enemies while he awaited his martyrdom. Here is one of his last prayers, written in his prison cell in the Tower of London.
Give me your grace, dear Lord ...
To think my worst enemies my best friends.
For the brothers of Joseph
could never have done him so much good with their love and favor
as they did him with their malice and hatred.

A Godly Meditation

St. Augustine once recounted an incident from the early life of his mother, St. Monica (c. 331-87). What was the moral of the story she had told him? Enemies, he concluded, may correct us.

A love of wine, she told me, began to creep up on her. She had been a sober girl, but her parents used to have her fetch them wine out of the cask in the cellar each day, and when she did, she would dip a cup in the opening at the top before she filled the pitcher. Then she would take just a tiny sip on the tip of her lips—the taste of it kept her from drinking any more than that.... But by adding to that tiny sip another tiny sip each day ... she fell into the habit of guzzling her little cups filled almost to the brim....

My God, what did you do when all this happened? How did you heal her? From which source did you bring her a remedy? You pulled out from another person's heart a rebuke, hard and sharp like a knife from your surgeon's bag—and in one stroke you cut away from her soul all that corrupt matter.

It just so happened that one day a maidservant who used to go with her down to the cellar quarreled with her young mistress when the two of them were alone. In anger, the maidservant flung this fault into her face with bitter insults, calling her a drunkard. Pierced all the way through by this taunt, she saw the terrible state she was in. Right away she condemned her own behavior and put a stop to it.

Just as flattering friends may ruin us, contentious enemies often correct us.

Confessions

If you don't forgive your enemies and allow them to refine you, what price will you pay? In God's eyes, says St. Augustine, the damage you inflict on yourself through a grudge is worse than anything your offender could possibly have done to you.

Whoever hates another person can only end up injuring himself most of all. For when you try to hurt the other person outwardly, you devastate yourself inwardly. To the degree that our soul is of more value than our body, to that same degree we ought to provide for it all the more, to protect it from harm. But whoever hates another person harms his own soul.

What exactly would you want to do to the person you hate? He may have taken away your money, but can he take away your faith? He may have wounded your reputation, but can he wound your conscience? Whatever injury he does to you is only external.

Now consider, on the other, what kind of injury you would inflict on yourself by your continuing hatred. For whoever hates another person is an enemy to himself within, even though he may not realize it.... Just suppose you injure your enemy. What's the result?

By this injury, he is damaged—but you become wicked. What a great difference there is between the two! He has lost only his money; you have lost your innocence. Tell me: Who has suffered the heavier loss? He lost something that was sure to perish anyway, while you have become someone who himself must now perish.

Homilies on New Testament Lessons

God sees every situation in the light of eternity. We must view our offenders, says St. Thomas More, from the same eternal perspective, keeping in mind our ultimate destiny. Knowing that death is hastening to snatch us away, who has time to be upset over the loss of things that pass so quickly away?

Who could be angry over the loss of goods if he remembers well how short a time he gets to keep them in the first place—how soon death might take them from him? Who could esteem himself so highly that he would take to heart a vile rebuke spoken to his face if he remembered who he really is: a poor prisoner condemned to death? Or how could we become so angry as we do now whenever someone does us bodily injury, if we were to think deeply about how we are indeed already laid in the executioner's cart?...

If we consider that this life is only a pilgrimage, and that we have no permanent dwelling place here, how foolish it is to scold and fight over little things along the way!... If we should see two men fighting together over serious matters, we would think them both crazy if they did not leave off fighting when they saw a ferocious lion coming toward them, ready to devour them both. Now considering that we surely see that death is coming on us all, and will undoubtedly within a short time devour us all—how soon, we don't know—isn't it worse than insanity to be angry and bear malice to one another, more often than not over trivial matters, in the same way children fight over cherry stones?

Treatise on the Last Things

Make sure your treasure is in heaven, says St. Aphraates (d. c. 345), the abbot known as the "Persian sage." Then earthly treasure won't mean much to you, and you won't be offended by those who take it from you.

The sons of peace remember death; and they forsake and remove from them wrath and enmity. As sojourners they dwell in this world, and prepare for themselves a provision for the journey before them. On that which is above they set their thoughts, on that which is above they meditate; and those things which are beneath their eyes they despise. They send away their treasures to the place where there is no peril, the place where there is no moth, nor are there thieves. They abide in the world as aliens, sons of a far land; and look forward to be sent out of this world and to come to the city, the place of the righteous.

Of Death and the Latter Times

Facing an unjust execution at the orders of his old friend, King Henry VIII, St. Thomas More wrote this meditation. Don't just think of your own fate at God's hands, he counsels; think of what lies ahead for your enemies as well. You'll find that it's only reasonable to love them, or at the very least, to pity them.

Bear no malice nor evil will to any living man. For the man is either good or evil. If he is good, and I hate him, then I am evil. If he is evil, then either he will repent and die good, and go to God, or he will remain evil, and die evil, and go to the devil. So then let me remember that if he is saved, and if I am saved too (as I trust to be), then he will in heaven not fail to love me quite heartily, and I shall then in the same way love him.

Why then should I now hate someone for this little while on earth who will in the hereafter love me forever? And why then should I now be an enemy to someone with whom I will eventually be joined in eternal friendship? On the other hand, if he should remain evil and be damned, then he is facing such an outrageous, eternal sorrow that I would rightly think myself a mortally cruel wretch if I would not now rather pity his pain than speak evil of him.... We should always pray, then, for the kind of merciful repentance in other folks that our own conscience shows us we need ourselves.

A Godly Instruction

TEN

"THE MINISTRY OF RECONCILIATION"
Practical Tips for Making Peace

All this is from God, who through Christ reconciled us to himself and gave us the ministry of reconciliation.

St. Paul
2 CORINTHIANS 5:18

Nothing is so characteristically Christian as being a peacemaker, and for this reason our Lord has promised us peacemakers a very high reward.

St. Basil
Epistles

Though we may often think of the saints as folks with their heads in the clouds, most of them have had their feet planted firmly on earth. In regard especially to the spiritual and moral dynamics of life, they have tended to be eminently practical men and women whose long conversations with God, long hours of self-examination, and long, hard experience with other struggling Christians has yielded shrewd insights.

Dealing with injuries and enemies is no simple task. The vague platitudes parroted in our contemporary culture are often less than helpful in this matter, and sometimes even harmful: "Just forgive and forget"; "Don't let them get the best of you"; "They'll get theirs; what goes around, comes around." In contrast, the wisdom of the saints on this subject provides advice that is at the same time more concrete and more spiritually profound.

Guidelines for Forgiveness

When people have approached the saints, seeking counsel about how to forgive and be reconciled, what useful tips have they received? In the last chapter we heard their recommendations about how to seek God's perspective on our conflicts as a way of preparing us to forgive. Once that foundation is laid, they suggest, the process of forgiveness and reconciliation can move forward if we follow a few simple guidelines.

To forgive truly, says St. Augustine, you must renounce the desire for revenge.

Now do not think that anger is insignificant.... And what is anger? The desire for revenge. Imagine: We desire to be avenged, when even Christ himself has not yet been avenged, nor have the martyrs been avenged. The patience of God still waits, so that the enemies of Christ, the enemies of the martyrs, might be converted. So who are we, that we should seek vengeance?

If God should seek vengeance against us for our own offenses, where could we hide? Even the One who has never done us harm in any way does not seek vengeance against us—yet are we seeking to be avenged, we who almost daily are offending God? So forgive; forgive from the heart.

Homilies on First John

A young monk who was injured by a brother complained to his abbot, St. Sisois of Thebes (fourth century). Here's how the wise old saint persuaded the youth to renounce his desire for vengeance.

"I want vengeance on a brother who has hurt me," the young monk declared.

The elder begged him: "Don't do that, my son; leave vengeance in God's hands."

But the younger man refused. "I can't rest," he insisted, "until I have revenge."

"Well, then, brother," said St. Sisois, "let's pray together."

The abbot stood up and said: "O God, since we are taking vengeance into our own hands, we have no further need even to think about you."

When the young monk heard the abbot's prayer, he fell at his feet and cried: "I won't quarrel with my brother any more! I beg you, forgive me."

Sayings of the Fathers

Don't delay, says St. John Chrysostom; forgive immediately.

If anger should ever cramp the soul, let it pass away quickly, and never last beyond a day. For "do not let the sun," says the apostle, "go down on your anger" [Eph 4:26]. If you're reconciled before evening, you'll obtain some pardon from God. But if you remain longer at enmity, that enmity can no longer be blamed on your being suddenly carried away by anger and resentment. Instead, it must be attributed to wickedness, and a foul spirit, and a soul that makes a practice of malice!

Meanwhile, depriving yourself of God's pardon isn't the only terrible thing you'll suffer. In addition, the right course of action will become still more difficult. For when one day is past, the shame becomes greater; and when the second has arrived, it's increased even further; and if it extends to a third and a fourth day, it will last into a fifth. Thus the five become ten; the ten, twenty; the twenty a hundred; and from then on the wound will become incurable—for as time goes on, the breach becomes wider.

So don't give way to any of these irrational passions. Don't be ashamed or blush, thinking, "A short time ago we called each other such names, and said a vast number of things fit or not fit to be spoken; how could I hurry now at once to seek a reconciliation? Won't everyone think I'm being too easy on him?"

I answer, no one who has any sense will blame you for being too easy on him; but if you remain implacable, then everyone will criticize you. That will give the devil the advantage of a wide breach between you and your offender. For then the enmity becomes more difficult to end, not merely because of the time elapsed, but also because of circumstances that take place in the meanwhile. Just as "love covers a multitude of sins" [1 Pt 4:8], so enmity, if given time, gives birth to new sins, putting a stamp of approval on those who make accusations, who enjoy seeing others suffer, and who tell the whole world about your disgraceful conduct.

Homilies on the Statues

It really doesn't matter who first caused offense, St. John Chrysostom adds; take the initiative in seeking reconciliation.

Some consider it a disgrace to be the first to make efforts at reconciliation. But tell me, what is shameful about being the first to make a spiritual profit? On the contrary, you ought to be ashamed of persisting in your anger, waiting until the person who has committed the injury comes to you to be reconciled. For this is the true disgrace, a reproach, the greatest loss of all.

Whoever takes the initiative in reconciliation reaps all the spiritual fruit. If you don't put aside your anger until the other person asks you to do so, then the good work is added to his account, rather than yours; for in that case, all you've done is to follow the law as if you were doing a favor to him, rather than obeying God. But instead, even when no one asks you, even when the one who has injured you fails to approach you or solicit your forgiveness, you should dismiss all thoughts of shame or reluctance, running forward freely to the injurer, so you can quell the anger entirely. If you do, the good deed becomes wholly your own, and you will receive all the reward....

Were you to see a limb of your body cut off, wouldn't you do everything in your power so that it could be reunited to your body? Make the same efforts with regard to your brothers when you see them cut off from your friendship. Hurry as fast as you can to be reconciled! Don't wait for them to make the first advance, but take the initiative yourself, so that you may be the first to receive the prize.

Homilies on the Statues

St. Jerome (c. 342-420) was known for his quick temper. After a dispute with his aunt, Castorina, who lived at some distance away, he took the initiative to seek peace by writing her letters.

The apostle and evangelist John rightly says, in his first epistle, that "anyone who hates his brother is a murderer" [1 Jn 3:15]. For, since murder often springs from hate, the hater, even though he has not yet slain his victim, is at heart a murderer. Why, you ask, do I begin in this style? Simply that you and I may both lay aside past ill feeling and cleanse our hearts to be a habitation for God.

"Be angry," David says, "but sin not" [Ps 4:4]—or, as the apostle more fully expresses it, "do not let the sun go down on your anger" [Eph 4:26]. What then shall we do in the day of judgment—we upon whose wrath the sun has gone down not one day but many years?

The Lord says in the Gospel: "If you are offering your gift at the altar, and there remember that your brother has something against you, leave the gift there before the altar and go; first be reconciled to your brother, and then come and offer your gift" [see Mt 5:23-24]. Woe to me, wretch that I am; woe, I had almost said, to you as well. According to this verse, for this long time past we have either offered no gift at the altar or have offered it while cherishing anger "without a cause" [see Mt 5:22; see RSV marginal note].

How have we been able in our daily prayers to say, "Forgive us our debts as we forgive our debtors," while our feelings have been at variance with our words, and our petition inconsistent with our conduct? Therefore I renew the prayer that I made a year ago in a previous letter, that the Lord's legacy of peace may be indeed ours, and that my desires and your feelings may find favor in his sight.

Soon we shall stand before his judgment seat to receive the reward of harmony restored or to pay the penalty for harmony broken. In case you shall prove unwilling—I hope that it may not be so—to accept my advances, I for my part shall be free. For this letter, when it is read, will insure my acquittal.

Epistle to Castorina

Don't brood over an offense, warns St. John Chrysostom; you'll only be punishing yourself instead of the offender.

God continually exhorts us, saying, "Let none of you imagine evil in your hearts against his friend" and "let not a man devise evil in his heart against his brother" [Zech 8:17, 7:10, Douay-Rheims]. He doesn't say merely to avoid anger, but not to keep it in your heart—don't think about it, let go of all your resentment, heal the inner sore.

If you brood over the injury, you may think you're paying him back. But instead you're tormenting yourself, and setting up your rage as an executioner within every part of you, tearing up your own insides. For what can be more wretched than a perpetually angry man? Just as maniacs can never enjoy tranquility, so those who are resentful and hold grudges can never enjoy peace.

Such a person rages incessantly, daily intensifying the storm of his thoughts, calling to mind the offender's words and acts, and hating the very name of the person who has wronged him. Only mention his enemy, and he becomes furious at once, suffering considerable inward anguish. Should he by chance catch even a glimpse of him, he fears and trembles, as if encountering the worst of evils.

In fact, even if he only spies one of his offender's relatives, or just an article of his clothing, or his house, or the street he lives on, he's tormented by the sight of them all.... When there are those we hate and hold as our enemies, we are stung by all these things; and the strokes we endure from the sight of each one of them are frequent and continual. What is the need, then, of sustaining such a siege, such torment, and such punishment?

Homilies on the Statues

St. Dorotheos of Gaza (sixth century), a wise abbot known widely for his counsel, compares brooding over injuries to stoking an interior fire.

Someone who is lighting a fire first sets a spark to the tinder; this is some brother's provoking remark.... Of what consequence is that brother's remark? If you put up with it, the spark goes out; but if you go on thinking, "Why did he say that to me?"... you add a small bit of wood to the flame ... and you produce some smoke, that is, a disturbance of mind. This disturbance floods the mind with thoughts and emotions which stimulate the heart and embolden it to ... vengeance.

On Rancor or Animosity

In the Book of Pastoral Rule, *Pope St. Gregory the Great advises pastors on how to counsel their flocks. His advice for working through offenses: Don't seethe in silence; talk over your anger with those who have offended you.*

Often those who have been offended suffer from remaining silent because it leads to more damaging words rushing through their hearts. Thoughts seethe all the more in the mind from being corralled by the violent guard of an indiscreet silence. And for the most part, the words that we think multiply even more than the words that we might have spoken, since people who are brooding count themselves safe from being heard by others who might criticize what they're thinking....

Moreover, those who tend to remain silent are more likely, when they suffer some injustice, to develop a keener sense of pain from not speaking about what they are enduring. For if the tongue were to tell calmly the annoyances that have been caused, the pain would flow away from their consciousness. But sores that are scabbed over may be more painful than those that are open—when the pus that is hot inside is pressed out, the pain itself drains out and leads to healing.

Thus those who are silent more than they ought to be should know about this tendency. Otherwise, amid the annoyances they endure while they hold their tongue, they may aggravate the violence of their pain. They should be admonished that, if they love their neighbors as themselves, they should by no means keep from them the grounds on which they rightly blame them.

For the voice is like a medicine with a simultaneously healthy effect on both parties: The one who inflicts the injury has his bad conduct corrected, and the one who sustains the injury has the violent heat of his pain relieved by opening out the sore....

The tongue, therefore, is like a dog that should be discreetly curbed, not tied up fast.

On the other hand, sometimes trying to talk out a dispute seems most likely to generate more anger. As St. Augustine saw it, this was the case in his scholarly quarrel with St. Jerome. So he wrote a letter to his old adversary, suggesting that they must simply be content to forgive and go on.

If it should be possible for us to examine and discuss anything that will nourish our hearts, without any bitterness of discord, I entreat you: Let us address ourselves to this. But if it is not possible for either of us to point out what he may judge to need correction in the other's writings without being suspected of envy and regarded as wounding friendship, let us, having regard to our spiritual life and health, leave such conversation alone. Let us content ourselves with smaller attainments.

Epistle to St. Jerome

What if your adversary resists your efforts to be reconciled? Then keep trying, says St. John Chrysostom.

Don't tell me, "I've sought him out many times, I've begged, I've pleaded, but I haven't been able to reconcile him." Never give up until you have reconciled him.... God pleads with us every day, and we refuse to listen—yet he doesn't stop pleading. Shouldn't you do the same?...

Suppose that you've pleaded often and been turned away—well, then, for your efforts you'll obtain a larger reward. For the more contentious he is, and the more you persevere in pleading, the more is your reward increased.

Homilies on the Statues

Despite our best efforts, however, peace isn't always possible. In that case, counsels Pope St. Gregory the Great, we should maintain within ourselves a conciliatory attitude toward the other party.

St. Paul says, "If possible, so far as it depends upon you, live peaceably with all" [Rom 12:18]. He says "if possible" because he recognizes that the good cannot have peace with the bad.

Since peace cannot be established except on two sides, when the bad flee from it, the good ought to keep it in their innermost hearts. Thus St. Paul admirably said, "So far as it depends on you"—meaning that peace should remain in us even when it is repelled by the hearts of bad men. And such peace we truly maintain, when we treat the faults of the proud at once with charity and with persistent justice, when we love them and hate their vices.

Epistles

Even if your adversary refuses to make peace with you, notes St. Augustine, your efforts will have their reward from God.

If you are full of peace, then, you should offer this greeting, as Jesus said: "Peace be to this house! And if a son of peace is there, your peace shall rest upon him; but if not"—for perhaps no one of peace is there (in which case you have lost nothing)—"it shall return to you" [see Lk 10:5-6]. It shall return to you, even though it never departed from you.

For this is what Jesus means to say: It was to your benefit to have declared peace, although it has not at all profited the one who refused to receive it. You have not lost your reward just because he has remained empty of peace. Your reward will still be given you for your good will, for the charity you have displayed. The One who will reward you has given you assurance of his reward by that angelic voice: "Peace on earth to men of good will" [see Lk 2:14].

Homilies on the Gospels

St. John Vianney (1786-1859), the humble priest of an obscure parish in rural France, was widely admired for the practical, homespun wisdom of his homilies. In this sermon, "Repairing the Wrong Done," he reminded his flock that reconciliation involves more than forgiveness. Wherever possible, you must make restitution or reparations for your wrongdoing.

Having made satisfaction to God, we must then make satisfaction to our neighbor the wrong which ... we have done him.... If we have sinned against him by injurious words, then we must apologize to him and make our reconciliation with him.... If we have done any harm, we are obliged to repay as soon as we can; otherwise we will be gravely at fault. If we have neglected to do that, we have sinned and we must confess it.

If you have done wrong to your neighbor in his honor, as,

for instance, by scandalous talk, you are obliged to make up by favorable and beneficent talk for all the harm you have done to his reputation, saying all the good of him which you know to be true and concealing any which he may have and which you are not obliged to reveal. If you have calumniated your neighbor, you must go and find the people to whom you have said false things about him and tell them that what you have been saying is not true, that you are very grieved about it, and that you beg them not to believe it....

Consider, too, whether you have ever taken anything from a next-door neighbor and neglected to pay it back.... If you wish to have the happiness of having your sins forgiven, you must have nothing belonging to anyone else which you should and could pay back.

St. Gregory Nazianzen (c. 329-89) was a brilliant Doctor of the Church whose responsibilities as archbishop of Constantinople brought him into contact with countless wealthy Christians—some of whom had acquired their riches unethically. Even if the victims of their avarice had forgiven them, the archbishop insisted, restitution was obligatory.

Don't let baptism only move you to honorable acquisition of wealth, but let it teach you also how to lose honorably the wealth you already possess—that is, to make restitution of what you have wrongfully acquired. For what will it profit you if your sin has been forgiven you, but the loss you've inflicted on someone else isn't restored to the one you've injured? Two sins are on your conscience; the one, that you made a dishonest gain; the other, that you retained the gains. You received forgiveness for the one, but in respect of the other you're still in sin, because you still have possession of what belongs to someone else.

Oration on Holy Baptism

"The way to overcome the devil when he excites feelings of hatred for those who injure us," *says St. John Vianney,* "is immediately to pray for their conversion." *Our Lord prayed for his enemies even as they murdered him; countless saints have imitated his example.*

Here is a prayer of St. Thomas More for his enemies, written after he was condemned to die, just a few days before his execution.

Almighty God, take from me ... all feelings of anger, all desire for revenge, all desire for or delight in other folks' harm, all pleasure in provoking any person to wrath or anger, all delight in upbraiding others or insulting any person in their affliction and calamity....

Almighty God, have mercy on all who bear an evil will toward me, and who wish to harm me. By the kind of gentle, tender, merciful means that your infinite wisdom can best devise, grant to correct and redress both their faults and mine together, and make us saved souls in heaven together, where we may ever live and love together with you and your blessed saints—O glorious Trinity, for the sake of the bitter passion of our sweet Savior Christ, Amen.

A Devout Prayer

Despite her youth, eleven-year-old St. Maria Goretti (1890-1902) found the grace to forgive the assailant who tried to rape her, and finally murdered her.

On a summer day in 1902, Maria was dragged into a farmhouse by a teenage boy named Alessandro whose intent was sexual assault. "No, no, no!" she cried. "Don't touch me! God doesn't want it! It's a sin—you'll go to hell!"

Because she resisted with all her might, the attacker failed to rape her, but instead gagged her with a handkerchief, pulled out a knife, and stabbed her fourteen times. While the doctors were trying to save her life, she never complained of the pain, but she did express her concern about the fate of her attacker. "Oh, Alessandro," she said, "how unhappy you are! You will go to hell!"

Before the priest at her bedside gave her the Blessed Sacrament for the last time, he asked her whether she had forgiven the boy. Without hesitation, she answered: "Yes ... for the love of Jesus, I forgive him ... and I want him to be with me in paradise.... May God forgive him, because I have already forgiven him." She died soon after.

Alessandro was found guilty of Maria's murder and sentenced to thirty years in prison. During the first eight years of his imprisonment, he showed no signs of remorse. But one night he dreamed of Maria, standing in a flowery meadow, offering him some white lilies. A few days later, the local bishop came to visit him, and soon afterward he wrote the bishop a letter begging God's forgiveness for his crime.

Alessandro visited Maria's mother on Christmas Eve, 1936, and asked her forgiveness as well. She replied that she could hardly refuse him what Maria herself had granted. He experienced a genuine conversion and reformation, and eventually he joined the Franciscan Third Order.

A final word of advice from the monks of the ancient desert: To avoid offense, practice patience.

When St. Anub (fourth century), St. Poemen, and five other monks had to flee a barbarian invasion of their hermitage in Skete, they settled for a few days in an old, abandoned pagan temple in a distant town. St. Anub asked to be left alone for a week, and the other monks agreed to his request.

In the temple stood a stone statue. Every morning of that week, St. Anub rose at dawn and pelted the statue's face with stones. Then every evening he would say, "Forgive me." From a distance the other monks watched his odd behavior, but said nothing.

At the end of the week, St. Poemen said: "Abbot, I saw you casting stones at the statue every day and then doing penance to it. Surely a true Christian would not do that."

The elder monk replied: "I did it for your sakes. When the statue was pelted with stones, did it complain? Was it angry?"

"No," said St. Poemen.

"When I did penance before the statue," St. Anub continued, "was it disturbed? Did it say, 'I refuse to forgive you'?"

"No."

"We are seven brothers here," said St. Anub. "If we want to stay together, we must each become like this statue— undisturbed by the injuries done to it. If we are unwilling to do that, then we should go our separate ways now."

The other monks agreed to live together as St. Anub had insisted. And they remained in harmony as a community for the rest of their lives, in quiet and brotherly peace.

"MAKE ME AN INSTRUMENT OF YOUR PEACE"

A Final Prayer

Blessed are the peacemakers,
for they will be called children of God.
MATTHEW 5:9, NAB

Lord, make me an instrument of your peace.
Where there is hatred, let me sow love;
Where there is injury, let me sow pardon;
Where there is doubt, faith;
Where there is despair, hope;
Where there is darkness, light;
Where there is sadness, joy.
O divine Master, grant that I may not seek so much
To be comforted as to comfort;
To be understood as to understand;
To be loved as to love.
For it is in giving that we receive;
It is in forgiving that we are forgiven;
And it is in dying that we are born to eternal life.

St. Francis of Assisi (1182-1226)

SOURCES FOR THE WISDOM OF THE SAINTS

Adels, Jill Haak, ed. *The Wisdom of the Saints: An Anthology.* New York: Oxford, 1987.

Albert the Great. *On Union With God.* Flelinfach, Wales: Llanerch, 1915.

Armstrong, Regis J., and Ignatius C. Brady, trans. *Francis and Clare: The Complete Works.* New York: Paulist, 1982.

Ball, Ann. *Modern Saints: Their Lives and Faces.* 2 vols. Rockford, Ill.: TAN, 1983.

Bridget of Sweden. *Birgitta of Sweden: Life and Selected Revelations.* Marguerite Tjader Harris, ed. Albert Ryle Kezel, trans. New York: Paulist, 1990.

Catherine of Genoa. *Purgation and Purgatory: The Spiritual Dialogue.* Serge Hughs, ed. New York: Paulist, 1979.

Chadwick, Owen. *Western Asceticism.* Philadelphia: Westminster, 1958.

Chervin, Rhonda De Sola. *Quotable Saints.* Ann Arbor, Mich.: Servant, 1992.

Delaney, John J. *Pocket Dictionary of Saints.* New York: Doubleday, 1980.

Dorotheos of Gaza. *Discourses and Sayings.* Eric P. Wheeler, trans. Kalamazoo, Mich.: Cistercian, 1977.

Eymard, Peter Julian. *Holy Communion.* Clara Morris Rumball, trans. New York: Eymard League, 1940.

Foucauld, Charles de. *Spiritual Autobiography of Charles de Foucauld.* Denville, N.J.: Dimension Books, 1964.

Fulgentius of Ruspe. *Fulgentius: Selected Works.* Robert B. Eno, trans. Washington, D.C.: Catholic University of America, 1997.

Ghezzi, Bert. *Voices of the Saints: A Year of Readings.* New York: Doubleday, 2000.

Kowalska, Maria Faustina. *Diary: Divine Mercy in My Soul.* Stockbridge, Mass.: Marians of the Immaculate Conception, 1987.

Liguori, Alphonsus de. *The Complete Works of Saint Alphonsus de Liguori.* Euegen Grimm, ed. New York: Benziger, 1886.

More, Thomas. *The Complete Works of St. Thomas More.* Garry E. Haupt, ed. 21 vols. New Haven, Conn.: Yale University Press, 1976.

Newman, John Henry. *John Henry Newman: Selected Sermons.* Ian Ker, ed. New York: Paulist, 1994.

The Office of Readings According to the Roman Rite. Boston: Daughters of St. Paul, 1983.

Prosperio, Leo. *St. Gemma Galgani.* Milwaukee, Wis.: Bruce, 1940.

Roberts, Alexander, and James Donaldson, eds. *The Ante-Nicene Fathers: The Writings of the Fathers Down to A.D. 325.* 10 vols. Grand Rapids, Mich.: Eerdmans, 1987 (reprint).

Sales, Francis de. *Introduction to the Devout Life.* New York: Wagner, 1923.

Schaff, Philip, ed. *A Select Library of the Nicene and Post-Nicene Fathers of the Christian Church.* 1st series, 14 vols. Grand Rapids, Mich.: Eerdmans, 1988 (reprint).

Schaff, Philip, and Henry Wace, eds. *A Select Library of the Nicene and Post-Nicene Fathers of the Christian Church.* 2d series, 14 vols. Grand Rapids, Mich.: Eerdmans, 1986 (reprint).

Teresa of Avila. *The Collected Works of St. Teresa of Avila.* Kieran Kavanaugh and Otilio Rodriguez, trans. 2 vols. Washington, D.C.: Institute of Carmelite Studies, 1980.

Thigpen, Paul, ed. *Be Merry in God: 60 Reflections From the Writings of St. Thomas More.* Ann Arbor, Mich.: Servant, 1999.

Thigpen, Paul, ed. *A Dictionary of Quotes From the Saints.* Ann Arbor, Mich.: Servant, 2001.

Thigpen, Paul, ed. *Restless Till We Rest in You: 60 Reflections From the Writings of St. Augustine.* Ann Arbor, Mich.: Servant, 1999.

Vianney, Jean-Baptiste. *The Sermons of the Curé of Ars.* Una Morrisy, trans. Chicago: Regnery, 1960.